ANGER MANAGEMENT WORKBOOK FOR MEN

ANGER MANAGEMENT WORKBOOK

—— *for* ——
MEN

Take Control of Your Anger and
Master Your Emotions

AARON KARMIN, MA

Licensed Clinical Professional Counselor

ALTHEA
PRESS

CONTENTS

FOREWORD

ON RARE OCCASIONS, you meet someone in a profession who is doing exactly what he or she should be doing. My friend Aaron Karmin is one of those people. What Hank Aaron was to baseball, Keith Richards was to rock 'n' roll, and Robin Williams was to comedy, Aaron Karmin is to psychotherapy. He's a master of his domain, and I was thrilled when I learned he was writing a book on anger management for men. With this book, Aaron will have the opportunity to share with the rest of the world his knowledge, his set of therapeutic skills, his extensive experience of working with anger, and his wisdom. If anger has been a problem for you, let me be the first to congratulate you on finding the right book written by the right author.

I met Aaron 15 years ago, when we were both starry-eyed psychology graduate students. Today, as a US Navy psychologist, I have a clientele made up largely of young men, so anger is an issue I encounter in my sessions on a daily basis. Despite my extensive training and experience in the treatment of mental health conditions, there are still times when I reach out for consultation and advice. One of my greatest resources in these moments continues to be Aaron.

Aaron's experience with anger is second to none. He spent several years working for an anger clinic in Chicago. He has authored a blog on anger management for the last several years and has been asked to speak publicly about anger management a number of times. He also has a regular guest spot on a Chicago radio station. Aaron is as smart as they come and, while his insights are thoughtful and sometimes complex, he communicates his thoughts in a way that makes them clear and precise. He has a gentleness about him that is necessary for every effective clinician. He has a passion for what he does, and he uses his unique style of humor at exactly the right times.

Given how common anger is, it's amazing that many mental health providers know little about treating it. The idea of walking away and counting to 10 is as simplistic as it is unhelpful. I believe this book will serve as the antidote to that long-standing dilemma. Although this is intended to be a self-help book, I suspect that it will serve as a valuable resource for clinicians as well.

Working as a clinical psychologist, I frequently hear the following comment: "It must be really hard hearing everyone's problems all day. Where do you go when you need to vent?" When this question is asked, I again think of my old friend Aaron. He's a therapist's therapist, and I'm excited that you will be the next beneficiary of his talents.

NATHAN R. HYDES, PhD, ABPP

Silverdale, Washington

PREFACE

OVER THE PAST few decades, what epidemic has had the most dire effects on American men? Is it cancer? AIDS? Drug abuse? Heart disease?

None of the above—it's violence.

We're well acquainted with violence against women and children, and with how violence affects their lives. Much more than we tend to suspect, however, violence is also a direct threat to the health and well-being of men.

Every year, there are millions of acts of violence. Some of these acts kill men, often leaving widows and orphans in their wake. But even when a violent encounter doesn't prove fatal, a man can suffer for the rest of his life from chronic physical injuries or mental scars caused by the attack.

Public and private agencies are attempting to deal with the epidemic of violence in our country, but their sole focus seems to be preventing overt acts of violence—using medication when it works, or incarceration when it doesn't—as if violence was an unstoppable natural force, and as if it was enough to hold this force back by any means necessary. And yet that approach does nothing to identify or address the underlying issue that leads men to seek violent solutions to their problems.

Here are three simple facts:

1. Violence is almost always accompanied by anger.
2. Our country's epidemic of violence is not about senseless crime—it's about the consequences of anger.
3. Men have the power to control their anger.

To believe that men cannot control their anger is to see violence as an uncontrollable animal instinct. It's a claim criminals have been making since time immemorial to exempt themselves from the consequences of their selfish behavior. We need to debunk that claim if we hope to break the cycle of violence.

As a society, though, we deny that we have a problem with anger. Clinicians and bureaucrats have given the most extreme kind of anger a fancy 10-syllable name—intermittent explosive disorder, or IED. According to a 2006 article published in the *Archives of General Psychiatry*, more than 7 percent of people in the United States have experienced IED at some point in their lives, and it appears more often in men than in women. This means that men are more likely to respond to certain situations with inappropriate levels of anger, leading to road rage, for example, or to violence. All the same, a diagnosis of IED is relatively uncommon, and the criteria for the diagnosis are fairly vague. Moreover, the practice of making that diagnosis is consistent with the medicalization of innate feelings. Instead of diagnosing a man with IED, it would be perfectly possible for a clinician to observe that the man is behaving badly, needs to make better choices, and needs to take responsibility for his decisions. But that would mean identifying this man's primary issue as anger, not violence, and it appears that we'd rather keep denying our problem with anger, even though one consequence of that denial is our high rate of violence as a nation.

Anger is a part of life. It's an ordinary part of being human. In fact, most of the anger that leads to violence doesn't have a pathological origin. It's just normal anger gone to extremes.

Everybody gets angry. But no one should react to getting angry by committing an act of violence. Since you're reading this book, chances are that you see anger as having brought some trouble into your life. Maybe you've lost a job, your marriage, or a friendship. Maybe you've even felt suicidal because of such losses, and maybe you've used alcohol or drugs to cope. But what you probably don't realize is that there's something underneath the clear anger you've felt toward people and situations in your life. Underneath the overt anger that you turn outward is a covert, malignant anger toward yourself, and that's what prevents you from being as happy and successful as you want to be.

This book will teach you the skills to confront your problem with anger and manage your anger in nonaggressive ways. Reading it will give you access to resources and expert knowledge that can help you apply your new skills to the situations that arise in your daily life. When you learn how to manage your anger without aggression, you gain a sense of accomplishment and success. As you increase your self-confidence and self-control, you build more independence and greater competence. That's another way of saying that anger management builds self-respect and strengthens the most important and most overlooked relationship in your life—your relationship with yourself.

INTRODUCTION

WE KNOW THAT everyone gets angry, and it's also true that people deal with the experience of anger in different ways. But this book isn't about people in general. It's about men, and about how men can learn to manage their anger without resorting to aggression.

Some men suppress their angry feelings because they think anger isn't nice. Other men are aware of being angry but have a hard time letting people know—and then they get mad at themselves for not being able to express their anger. And other men are able to experience and express their anger, but feel guilty when they do.

Did you recognize yourself in one or more of those descriptions?

Because you have at least some level of interest in anger management, my guess is that you're not a bully. I'm guessing you love your family members and friends, even though you often hurt them as deeply as you care for them. And I'm guessing that you wonder why you do that.

There are probably a number of reasons for your hurtful expressions of anger, and you're probably not aware of them all. They may include early experiences of abuse and trauma or other painful experiences that continue to shape your perceptions. And no one would deny how important it is to identify and understand the impact of such factors. But the purpose of anger management is not really to dwell on the past. It's to identify what triggers explosive rage in the present. That's why this book focuses on teaching you how to discover what triggers your anger in the moment, and how to react to your anger in a constructive way.

To be clear, though, this book is not a substitute for mental health counseling. If you need more support than self-help can provide, I urge you to seek out a qualified professional (see the Resources section on page 146).

It's also important for you to understand that no circumstances ever make it all right for anyone to physically abuse you. If you can't walk away from a threatening situation and establish your physical safety, call the police right away.

And be aware that strong emotions are often associated with physical sensations—dizziness, a pounding heart, tingling, and other strong physiological responses. If you've been experiencing sensations like these, consider seeing a physician before you undertake the work of confronting your anger. Likewise, as you read this book, *stop reading immediately* if anything starts to feel too uncomfortable, and come back only when it feels safe and comfortable for you to continue.

When you do, you'll find the book includes many helpful features, including:

- Information about the purpose of anger, and about how to identify your anger
- Assessments to evaluate how angry you are
- Information about biological responses that trigger anger and about anger's impact on your body, moods, thoughts, and behavior
- Concrete examples of communicating and expressing anger in positive, productive ways
- Clinical examples of anger-management strategies, adapted from my work with clients in my counseling practice (names and other identifying details have been changed)

Ultimately, as you learn to manage your anger in a nonaggressive manner, you'll also be learning to accept yourself and care less about the dysfunctional opinions of others. Got all that? Good. Let's get started.

Defining and Recognizing Anger

Most people never learn a formal definition of anger, but they form personal definitions of anger from learning what it's like to feel angry and recognizing how others look when they're angry.

How do you define anger?

_____

_____

_____

_____

_____

_____

_____

_____

_____

_____

_____

_____

_____

_____

_____

_____

_____

_____

_____

— PART 1 —

ABOUT ANGER

1 WHAT IS ANGER?

There was once a little boy who had a bad disposition. His father gave him a bag of nails and a hammer and told him to drive a nail into the back fence every time he lost his temper. On the first day alone, the boy drove 37 nails into the fence.

Gradually the boy discovered that it was easier to keep his temper than to drive nails into the fence, and the day came when he didn't lose his temper at all. His father now suggested that the boy pull one nail out of the fence every time he was able to keep his temper. The days passed, and the boy was finally able to tell his father that all the nails were gone.

"You've done well," the boy's father said. "But look at all the holes in the fence! It will never be the same. When you say things in anger, your angry words leave scars just like these."

ANGER IS AN instinctual emotional response triggered by a real or imagined threat. Most men feel angry when someone or something obstructs them in some way. Anger is painful, and so we all seek relief from the feeling it brings. Lots of men respond to the feeling of anger by immediately wanting the satisfaction of forcing the "obstacle" out of the way—or, if it won't move, cursing or insulting it.

Most people, at one time or another, have experienced conflict between what they think and what they feel. For example, everything can appear to be running smoothly for a man as he drives to work. His feelings, thoughts, and behavior are all working in harmony toward the goal of arriving on time. But then another driver cuts him off, and he reacts in a way that seems out of character for him—an explosion of road rage, say, or some other kind of emotional meltdown. And even though his rational mind knows that his reaction is out of proportion to what happened, his emotions run away with him.

If out-of-control anger like that is an issue for you, it's a real problem. But suppressing anger is also problematic because, like every other emotion, it exists for a reason. When you discover the purpose that anger serves in your life, you put yourself in a position to understand your anger and manage its impact in constructive ways.

If you have trouble knowing or saying how you feel, then the relationship between your feelings and the events in your life is not going to be clear to you or others. In this chapter, we'll talk about what anger is, and we'll consider why men have special issues with anger. We'll also look at some common myths about anger, explore the five reasons why anger occurs, examine the four basic components of anger management, and discuss how and why we suppress anger. At the end of the chapter, you'll have an opportunity to discover, in objective terms, how problematic anger is for you.

What's Special About Men and Anger?

Many people don't understand why men behave in irrational ways when they're angry. At times it seems as if men just don't think things through. Compared to women, men are more likely to act impulsively, misread social cues, misinterpret others' emotions, get involved in physical fights, and engage in risky behavior. They're also less likely than women to think before they act, consider the consequences of their actions, and modify their behavior when it's inappropriate or even dangerous.

Take an Anger Inventory

Let's begin with an exercise that probes some of the history between you and anger. Think of a time when you felt really angry. Make sure that the incident you choose reflects your current relationship with anger. With that incident in mind, read through the following questions, and choose the responses that best describe when and where you got angry, what happened, and how you responded. If you want to, you can add comments and reflections.

When?

Date _____

☐ Morning ☐ Afternoon ☐ Evening ☐ Night

Comments _____

_____

_____

_____

_____

_____

Where?

☐ At home ☐ At work ☐ In the community

Somewhere else _____

_____

_____

_____

_____

_____

What happened?

- ☐ Somebody said something
- ☐ You did something wrong
- ☐ Somebody treated you unfairly
- ☐ Something else _____

☐ Somebody did something
☐ Somebody bossed you around
☐ You did not get what you wanted

_____

_____

_____

_____

_____

What did you do?

- ☐ Yelled ☐ Cursed ☐ Behaved in a violent way
- ☐ Walked away ☐ Made an assertive statement
- ☐ Threw something ☐ Talked to somebody about your anger
- ☐ Did something mean to the person later
- ☐ Something else _____

_____

_____

_____

_____

_____

If you are patient in one moment of anger, you will escape a hundred days of sorrow.

Men are generally larger than women, and as a result they have bigger heads. But that doesn't make men smarter than women, according to Louann Brizendine, author of *The Male Brain*. Women's brains are smaller than men's, but the female brain has a higher processing capacity. In fact, men's brains take longer to mature than women's do, and the prefrontal cortex of the brain—the center of reasoning and judgment and the part of the brain that modulates aggression—is smaller and develops more slowly in men than in women, as Sandra Aamodt and Sam Wang explain in their book *Welcome to Your Child's Brain*. A 2014 study published in the journal *Violence and Gender* identified this difference as one reason for men's tendency to express more anger than women.

TRAITS OF THE "TOUGH GUY"

Tough guys look strong, but what appears to be strength is actually overcompensation for feelings of inferiority and inadequacy. And tough guys don't demonstrate manliness in other ways—by making useful contributions to their communities, for example, or by being cooperative husbands and setting appropriate examples for their children to follow.

They tend to see emotions as strictly for women and sissies, and they suffer from a lifelong inability to enjoy loving, supportive relationships. Men who subscribe to the "tough guy" mentality also tend to confuse the following things:

- Cooperation and submission
- Mistakes and weakness
- Machismo and strength
- Conceit and confidence
- Isolation and independence
- Interdependence and dependence
- Irresponsibility and freedom
- Self-indulgence and happiness

For many tough guys, these traits are carryovers from their youth. The antidote to their role as tough guys or macho men is time. With time they age and are forced to find other, more appropriate and mature means of defining themselves in the world. And many alumni of Tough Guy Academy have indeed managed to outgrow these immature traits and become self-respecting adults.

Men and women also respond differently to signals from the amygdala, the part of the brain where fear arises. Women's responses to these signals are different from men's because the female brain evolved in such a way that our female ancestors learned to seek safety in groups, and to reduce stress by connecting with others. Women's hormones are also dominated by estrogen, and so women have less testosterone and more estrogen flowing through their brains. The evolution of the female brain, together with women's biological makeup, generally makes it easier for a woman to look for a solution to a conflict, even if she may have to compromise and make some personal sacrifices to resolve the situation. Our female ancestors may have had to compete, sometimes for mates and sometimes for food, but their primary goals were social support and the care and protection of children.

Men, by contrast, are programmed to compete so they can reproduce and pass on their genes. Our male ancestors were hunter-gatherers, and that work called for aggression as well as rules that fostered hierarchy, competition, and dominance. And the testosterone that bathes the male brain promotes social withdrawal and the desire to be left alone. From a biological standpoint, a man is relatively uninterested in conversation because testosterone decreases his desire to socialize, except when competition makes socialization necessary or when he is in pursuit of sex. Testosterone also tells a man that dominance and control are the way to safety, and so he's hardwired to experience challenges to his independence and authority as stressors. He has a biological drive to seek respect and find his place in the pecking order through dominance and aggression. Moreover, the male amydgala has a high concentration of sex hormone receptors, including testosterone, that heighten these responses, a fact believed to explain why men are more prone than women to displays of anger, and why men's stress reactions quickly escalate to conflict. Men don't look for social connection the way women do.

Men's and women's stances toward social connection appear to be another hardwired characteristic. In *The Female Brain,* Louann Brizendine cites researchers who found that baby boys in the first three months of life looked around to investigate their environments but rarely glanced at their mothers, whereas baby girls of the same age made more eye contact with their mothers and focused more frequently on faces. Women tend to have greater ability than men to read faces, a characteristic that enabled our female ancestors not only to interpret what others needed but also to anticipate others' behavior so that they could protect themselves and their children.

In short, women's brains are programmed for social harmony, and men's brains are programmed for social hierarchy backed by competition and dominance. But this doesn't mean that men can't make good decisions, tell the difference between right and wrong, or learn to manage their anger. Biology may account for certain tendencies, but men have the power to counteract those tendencies with self-control and healthy choices.

Common Myths About Anger

I want you to know that participating in anger management is not a sign of weakness or failure. Seeking support is a sign of strength, not weakness. We all need help from time to time, and it's a sign of intelligence to know when to ask for support and guidance. Besides, we get professional support for all kinds of issues, from a leaky faucet to a complicated tax return, and anger is no different. Controlling your anger is a skill that you can learn.

But if you're like a lot of other men, you may have come to believe certain myths about anger. Sometimes these myths excuse anger or make it seem like the only possible response to a situation. As you learn to manage your anger without aggression, it will be important for you to reflect on such myths and challenge them.

MYTH 1: YOU INHERITED YOUR ANGER

If your father was an angry man, maybe you think you inherited your anger from him. But that's just another way of saying that your anger is something you can't change. You may have been born with a tendency to become angrier than other people, but what really matters is how you *react* to the experience of becoming angry. That is learned behavior, and you can change it. And when you take ownership of your reactions to anger, you become responsible for your own happiness because you make your happiness the product of your own choices, not something that depends on other people's behavior.

The Biology of You

Knowledge is power, so don't be afraid to consider the biological side of who you are. As a man, you have certain advantages and disadvantages due to the biological characteristics of your brain. (The same is true for women, of course.) Understanding the biological basis of who you are can help you use those advantages, compensate for the disadvantages, and make changes that will enhance your ability to succeed in your present environment.

What advantages does anger have for you?

_____

_____

_____

_____

_____

_____

_____

_____

What disadvantages does anger have for you?

_____

_____

_____

_____

_____

_____

_____

_____

MYTH 2: ANGER WILL HURT YOU IF YOU DON'T EXPRESS IT QUICKLY AND FORCEFULLY

If you believe this myth, then it will seem to you that it's healthy to "blow your top" and lose your temper the minute something goes wrong. But people often feel much worse after losing control over their angry feelings. Shouting, hitting, and slamming doors all increase and strengthen feelings of anger. At the same time, you don't do yourself or anyone else any favors by keeping your anger completely to yourself, but you probably can't do that anyway. If you're angry, you may show it by sulking or having a certain tone in your voice—this kind of behavior is called *passive aggression*. People around you know that you're angry, but they don't know why you're angry. When you learn to express your anger in constructive ways, you promote deeper involvement with other people.

MYTH 3: LOVE AND ANGER DON'T MIX

To believe that love and anger don't mix is to believe that you should never feel anger toward someone you love—and that if you're in conflict with someone you don't know or don't like, then you're a wimp if you *don't* get angry. But it's important to understand that anger typically occurs in degrees. It ranges from mild annoyance to intense rage. If you don't know how to recognize and name the degrees of your anger, then you may see even slight irritation as an intense, urgent crisis. The antidote to being out-of-control angry is learning to be firm, sure, and in control—that is, learning to be *assertive*.

MYTH 4: GETTING MAD IS A GOOD WAY TO MAKE OTHERS BEHAVE

This myth depends on the idea that other people are universally dangerous and that anger is a good way to protect yourself and those you care about. That may have been true at a particular time in your life, but continuing to believe this myth can cause problems. After all, good friendships are not based on fear, and it is unlikely that you will have successful relationships if you exhibit angry behavior. In fact, others will see you as threatening and may pick fights with you if you seem like an angry person. Anger doesn't have to be your go-to solution for every problem you encounter and every danger you face. There's usually a better way, and you can trust your judgment to find the right approach as problems present themselves.

MYTH 5: ANGER IS JUSTIFIED BY OTHER PEOPLE'S BAD BEHAVIOR

This myth is often perpetuated by people who have been victims of violence or aggression. Anger is a natural reaction to being taken advantage of or mistreated. But if it permeates every area of your life, it can cause difficulties. It is better to tackle past hurt in ways that don't involve exchanging one unpleasant emotion, such as fear or loss, for anger or rage.

MYTH 6: ANGER IS DESTRUCTIVE AND UNHEALTHY

This myth expresses the belief that anger is an abnormal state, a deviation from "normal" serenity. In fact, anger is a common, garden-variety emotion. A truly normal emotional state is one in which feelings are continuously flowing and changing. Anger is as much a part of that flow as happiness, sadness, or any other feeling. It is a natural response, and there are times when it's definitely justified and appropriate—for example, in response to a friend's betrayal, a physical attack, or a major social injustice. But a temper tantrum over a minor irritation is both destructive and unhealthy. If anger is expressed when it's first felt, it subsides. If it is suppressed, it often grows stronger. Feelings are better expressed with words ("Waiting in line makes me angry") than with behavior (punching or shouting). And it's okay to wait until you feel composed before confronting someone you're angry with.

> **A truly normal emotional state is one in which feelings are continuously flowing and changing. Anger is as much a part of that flow as happiness, sadness, or any other feeling.**

Mythbusting

This exercise poses some questions intended to help you determine whether you've been affected by one or more myths about anger. As you answer the questions, think about how they may point to ways of getting beyond these common myths.

What makes you happy?

_____

_____

_____

_____

_____

How do you behave when you're angry?

_____

_____

_____

_____

_____

How do you behave when someone you love behaves in a way that frustrates, irritates, or hurts you?

_____

_____

_____

_____

_____

How do you behave when a stranger or someone you don't like behaves in a way that you find annoying or offensive?

_____

_____

_____

_____

_____

What is your anger trying to achieve?

_____

_____

_____

_____

_____

What triggers your anger?

_____

_____

_____

_____

_____

What's the worst part about your anger?

_____

_____

_____

_____

_____

Five Reasons Anger Occurs

Try looking at anger in terms of the following five reasons for angry behavior, which are driven by particular feelings:

1 **Seeking revenge.** You feel hurt, so you want to get even and make things fair.
2 **Preventing disaster.** You feel helpless, so you want to take control.
3 **Pushing others away.** You feel discouraged, so you want to withdraw from life and avoid being judged.
4 **Getting attention.** You feel disrespected, so you lash out to be acknowledged or to prove your importance.
5 **Expressing difficult feelings.** You're overwhelmed, so you want to reduce your discomfort.

Four Keys to Managing Anger

Managing your anger means not saying or doing things you'll later regret. It means calming yourself, assessing situations with a cool head, and taking sensible actions. It basically involves making choices around four components of your behavior:

1 Expressing yourself
2 Taking care of yourself
3 Building up your tolerance for frustration
4 Maintaining a positive outlook

EXPRESSING YOURSELF

When you express yourself, you *promote constructive communication.* Have you ever heard the expression that communication is 10 percent information and 90 percent emotion? It means that good communication is more than just sending a message. It's like a game of catch. It involves making sure that the message you send someone else is the message they've received, and that the message you receive is the message the other person has sent. Easier said than done!

Reasons for Anger

Which of these purposes does anger serve in your life?

_____

_____

_____

_____

_____

_____

_____

_____

_____

_____

_____

_____

_____

_____

_____

_____

_____

_____

_____

ANGER: THE UPSIDE Anger motivates us to change because it encourages us to take necessary and appropriate action. It confirms our individuality because it promotes our independence. It helps us protect ourselves from threats and dangers. And it focuses our attention on problems, giving us the energy to solve them and helping us concentrate on finding solutions.

Communication is effective and constructive when actions match words. If your words and actions don't match, then your listener will ask you for clarity, and you will need to offer it. So as you talk with someone, pay attention to how you're feeling, to the words you're using, and to what your body language may be saying.

Because communication is a two-way street, expressing yourself effectively also means listening to your partner in a conversation. For example, if your wife is saying the same thing over and over, maybe she thinks her emotions haven't been heard along with her words. That's a common issue because it's so easy for a listener to jump over someone's feelings and start giving advice, sharing facts, or trying to minimize a problem instead of really hearing what the other person is saying. But when you refuse to hear someone else's feelings, you're saying, in effect, "Your feelings are not okay. You have no right to feel that way." And when you verbally attack other people, they respond by defending themselves and counterattacking, and pretty soon the discussion has escalated into something so completely unrelated to honest emotional needs that further talking can't lead to a solution.

This works the other way, too—if you're not fully heard, then you can't communicate your needs. So it's understandable that you feel frustrated or angry when you're not feeling heard and the other person just cuts you off by saying, "That's ridiculous!" You can't solve a problem that you don't understand, and full communication—listening to words while also listening for feelings—is what leads to understanding. Surprisingly, though, there's often no need to solve the problem, whatever it is, once the people discussing it are sure that their feelings have been heard.

TAKING CARE OF YOURSELF

When you take care of yourself, you *promote your own happiness*. Your happiness is just as important as anyone else's, so set some limits on others' demands. Your whole day doesn't have to be a round of people-pleasing tasks. Today maybe someone else can pick up the dry cleaning or mow your mother's lawn.

Again, though, this is easier said than done. People who want you to do things for them may think you're being selfish if you say no, and you may think so yourself.

But this is really more about self-preservation. How can you truly care for others if you don't care for yourself first? Besides, why not be a role model for self-care? Otherwise, all you'll be doing is teaching others that you'll always be there to solve their problems, and they'll never learn to do that themselves. It may be hard to set boundaries and then watch people struggle, but that's how people grow.

BUILDING UP YOUR TOLERANCE FOR FRUSTRATION

When you increase your tolerance for frustration, you *foster forgiveness*. If someone hurts you—a neighbor tells lies about you behind your back, your business partner steals from you, your spouse has an affair—you want to lash out in anger, especially if the other person's behavior involves a personal betrayal, or if there's a significant difference in power between you and the person who hurt you.

When you can't hit back, your frustration can feel extreme. Why shouldn't you seek revenge? Why should you ever forgive anyone who betrays you? These are legitimate questions. And the answers have to do with an important fact: *Forgiving someone else's bad behavior is not the same thing as forgetting or condoning the behavior.*

Forgetting means repressing—bottling up hurt and anger. But forgiveness is a powerful stance because it rests on the ability to let go of your painful feelings about a person or an event so you can move on with your life. Someone else's bad behavior caused you pain, and you are making the choice to let your anger and pain go. Forgiving others' hurtful behavior is an opportunity for you to let them be responsible for themselves.

Your act of forgiveness is for your benefit, not anyone else's. As the old saying goes, holding a grudge against someone is like drinking poison and waiting for the other person to die. When you seek revenge or wish harm to another, the bitterness of your feelings depletes your energy and prevents your pain from healing. But when you increase your tolerance for frustration—that is, your tolerance for not lashing out when others hurt or disappoint you—you can learn more about the world and discover new opportunities to grow and stay healthy, because you've developed the power to let go of the past and enjoy your life in the present.

MAINTAINING A POSITIVE OUTLOOK

When you maintain a positive outlook, you become more able to *manage your interpretation of events*. Your outlook on life—its specific events and the other people involved in them—has much more to do with how you feel than it does with actual events and people in your life. If you see the world as a terrible place where the cards are stacked against you, then you create a formula for anger, sadness, or worry. You have a choice about what you emphasize in the world around you. If you wake up in the morning and it's raining, you can interpret that fact as a personal affront from nature and bemoan the gray, depressing day to come. Or, you can look out at the rain and feel content to be warm and dry in your comfortable home. It's really up to you.

Instant Gratification

Your ability to manage your interpretation of an event is crucially dependent on your ability to delay gratification.

Men used to be brought up in conditions where some level of hardship was normal. Thrift used to be an essential aspect of middle-class life, and the things people longed for were not instantly available—they had to be earned. As a result, people appreciated and placed much more attention on what they had than on what they lacked. There was a sense of pride in mastery, and a feeling of achievement in having reached a goal through hard work and struggle.

By contrast, many modern men grew up in circumstances where instant gratification was the norm. When they were children they were showered with toys, fed whatever they wanted whenever they wanted it, and provided with entertainment instead of having to look for it. They didn't have to wait for, earn, or create the things they wanted, and they didn't have to find alternatives if those things weren't available.

What happened to some of those children? They grew up to be men with serious impulse control and self-regulation issues. When they don't get the things they feel entitled to, they perceive themselves as being treated unfairly, and that perception triggers exaggerated outbursts of anger.

Managing Your Anger

This exercise will help you gauge your current ability to make constructive choices around the experience of feeling angry.

What is the hardest part of managing your anger when you are . . .?

Expressing yourself?

_____
_____
_____
_____

Taking care of yourself?

_____
_____
_____
_____

Tolerating frustration?

_____
_____
_____
_____

Maintaining a positive outlook?

_____
_____
_____
_____

No one would suggest that men today need more hardship or more obstacles to acquiring what they want and need, but there has to be a middle ground between suffering constant adversity and having everything now. That middle ground is where men develop maturity, which is all about discovering that they can't always have what they want, but they can still be healthy and happy.

If you've reached adulthood without having developed the skill of delaying gratification, you can focus now on developing that skill so as to reduce and manage impulse-related behavior throughout the rest of your life. For example, in a traffic jam or when you're not getting your needs met as a customer, you can use anger management to counterbalance the hostile, impulsive, infantile insistence on getting exactly what you want, exactly when you want it.

When have you had to wait for something you wanted?

_____

_____

_____

_____

What challenges have you overcome around getting what you wanted when you wanted it?

_____

_____

_____

_____

RESILIENCE The learning that comes from delaying gratification contributes to the growth of resilience. Resilient men can withstand setbacks, rise to a challenge, and find new ways of solving problems. They feel confident about managing the social and material worlds, and they know that hardship can be overcome.

How and Why We Suppress Anger

Just as you can choose how to interpret the events in your life, you have options for expressing your anger. But men often limit their options by erroneously reducing them to just two choices—expressing their anger in direct personal confrontations, or keeping their anger to themselves. But if you've ever been surprised by the intensity of your anger about something, or if you've ever been caught off guard by someone else's sudden and intense anger, then you know what suppressed anger looks like when it's finally expressed.

Anger is a naturally occurring emotion, and it's healthy to express anger when you do it in the right way and at the right time. But here's the key: *anger is a secondary feeling*. This means that before you get angry, you always feel something else first—fear, hopelessness, hurt, disappointment, or guilt, for example. Those are all emotions that are connected with feeling vulnerable, and lots of men use anger to cover up or protect themselves from those vulnerable feelings and from emotional pain. But suppressing anger is not the same as controlling anger. Suppressing anger just means stuffing it down rather than risking the consequences of letting it out.

When men have problems with anger, it's often because they're putting either too much or too little emphasis on it. Putting too much emphasis on anger compounds it. Too much emphasis strengthens anger and makes it worse. But putting too little emphasis on anger often leads to suppression not just of anger, but of other emotions as well. This can end in numbness, since cutting off the "bad" emotions also means not being able to feel the "good" ones. You lose touch with an important part of yourself. And in the worst-case scenario, your anger builds up to the point where it becomes explosive and may even be directed at someone who has nothing at all to do with why you're angry.

When we do not understand how to effectively deal with anger, we often choose coping methods that are harmful. Here are some unhelpful ways of coping with anger:

- **Putting anger down.** We deny anger or repress it. Some of us like to keep our "nice person" image and not make waves. Perhaps we say to ourselves that the situation is not important, and we swallow our anger.

- **Putting anger off.** We think we can put the situation off, not get angry, and deal with it later.
- **Transferring anger.** We are nice to people who make us angry, but we are hateful to those who love us. For example, a man's boss criticizes him at work, but the man takes his anger out on his child instead of expressing his anger to his boss. Or a man whose first wife cheated on him feels a rush of jealous anger toward his new wife when she says, "I might be late getting home tonight."
- **Deadening feelings.** People who can't cope with their anger and are afraid to express it often choose not to feel any emotions at all. Their reasoning is that if they don't feel anything, then they can't be hurt. This is a very dangerous method because it puts them out of touch with their emotional reality.
- **Staying in control.** Some people think that they must always be in control of a situation. They see anger as weakness and unthinkable loss of control.

We are not thinking machines that feel—we're feeling beings who think.

The Importance of Emotions

It's unfortunate that so many people distrust their emotions. People are often told to focus on objective facts instead of feelings. A pervasive distrust of emotion is evident in stock phrases like "Sorry—I wasn't thinking." Rarely does anyone say, "Sorry—I wasn't feeling."

It's true that strong feelings can interfere with clear thinking. But not being aware of your feelings interferes with your well-being.

Your feelings are related to both your mind and your body. Emotions are intangible, however. There is no one way to define a feeling. When you see someone crying, you have no way of knowing whether that person is in physical pain, overwhelmed by grief, or if they just finished slicing an onion. There is no single event or object to which everyone will have the same emotional response. That's why behavior alone is such a poor indicator of what someone else is feeling.

But men learn from other men, and one major lesson they teach each other is that behavior does a better job of conveying emotions than words. What many men don't know is that the expression of anger doesn't have to involve behaviors like yelling or hitting, just as the expression of sadness doesn't have to include crying, and the expression of fear doesn't have to mean hiding or running away.

Another myth many men teach each other is that some feelings are bad and others are good. In truth, however, feelings are neither good nor bad. Feelings just *are*. If you listen to your emotions and understand what they mean, then you can address them, and their intensity will fade. But if you ignore what your emotions are telling you, then your feelings build up, and you may eventually express them through destructive behavior.

Wouldn't it be wonderful if you could feel perfectly happy every moment of your life? But there's a word for animals that cannot feel anger, fear, and pain—*extinct*. Emotions have survival value. They may not make logical sense, but they're an unavoidable part of life, and they're part of being human.

For you, what is the worst thing about having emotions?

The Clinical Anger Scale

The Clinical Anger Scale (CAS), developed by William Snell, is considered the first reliable questionnaire to assess the symptoms of anger and measure the array of symptoms that constitute *clinical anger,* which is a term for anger that has become problematic and needs to be managed. The CAS measures symptoms in each of the following areas, in this order: anger in the present, anger about the future, anger about failure, anger about things, hostility, social interactions, anger about yourself, blame, violence, shouting at people, irritation, social activities, decision making, relationships, work, sleep, fatigue, appetite, health, concentration, and sex. Your answers to these items will show you the areas in which your anger arises.

As you complete the questionnaire, be honest with yourself. Read each item, and then circle the letter next to the response that best reflects how you feel most of the time in your current life. Choose only one response for each item.

1. A. I do not feel angry.

    B. I feel angry.

    C. I am angry most of the time now.

    D. I am so angry and hostile all the time that I can't stand it.

2. A. I am not particularly angry about my future.

    B. When I think about my future, I feel angry.

    C. I feel angry about what I have to look forward to.

    D. I feel intensely angry about my future, since it cannot be improved.

3. **A.** It makes me angry that I feel like such a failure.

   B. It makes me angry that I have failed more than the average person.

   C. As I look back on my life, I feel angry about my failures.

   D. It makes me angry to feel like a complete failure.

4. **A.** I am not all that angry about things.

   B. I am becoming more hostile about things than I used to be.

   C. I am pretty angry about things these days.

   D. I am angry and hostile about everything.

5. **A.** I don't feel particularly hostile toward others.

   B. I feel hostile a good deal of the time.

   C. I feel quite hostile most of the time.

   D. I feel hostile all of the time.

6. **A.** I don't feel that others are trying to annoy me.

   B. At times I think people are trying to annoy me.

   C. More people than usual are beginning to make me feel angry.

   D. I feel that others are constantly and intentionally making me angry.

7. **A.** I don't feel angry when I think about myself.

   B. I feel angrier about myself these days than I used to.

   C. I feel angry about myself a good deal of the time.

   D. When I think about myself, I feel intense anger.

8.   **A.**   I don't have angry feelings about others having screwed up my life.

     B.   It's beginning to make me angry that others are screwing up my life.

     C.   I feel angry that others prevent me from having a good life.

     D.   I am constantly angry because others have made my life totally miserable.

9.   **A.**   I don't feel angry enough to hurt someone.

     B.   Sometimes I am so angry that I feel like hurting others, but I would not really do it.

     C.   My anger is so intense that I sometimes feel like hurting others.

     D.   I'm so angry that I would like to hurt someone.

10.   **A.**   I don't shout at people any more than usual.

     B.   I shout at others more now than I used to.

     C.   I shout at people all the time now.

     D.   I shout at others so often that sometimes I just can't stop.

11.   **A.**   Things are not more irritating to me now than usual.

     B.   I feel slightly more irritated now than usual.

     C.   I feel irritated a good deal of the time.

     D.   I'm irritated all the time now.

12.   **A.**   My anger does not interfere with my interest in other people.

     B.   My anger sometimes interferes with my interest in others.

     C.   I am becoming so angry that I don't want to be around others.

     D.   I'm so angry that I can't stand being around people.

13. **A.** I don't have any persistent angry feelings that influence my ability to make decisions.

   B. My feelings of anger occasionally undermine my ability to make decisions.

   C. My anger regularly interferes with sound decision-making.

   D. I'm so angry that I can't make good decisions anymore.

14. **A.** I'm not so angry and hostile that others dislike me.

   B. People sometimes dislike being around me since I become angry.

   C. More often than not, people stay away from me because I'm so hostile and angry.

   D. People don't like me anymore because I'm angry all the time.

15. **A.** My feelings of anger do not interfere with my work.

   B. From time to time my feelings of anger interfere with my work.

   C. I feel so angry that it interferes with my capacity to work.

   D. My feelings of anger prevent me from doing any work at all.

16. **A.** My anger does not interfere with my sleep.

   B. Sometimes I don't sleep very well because I'm feeling angry.

   C. My anger is so great that it keeps me up one to two hours later than usual.

   D. I am so intensely angry that I can't get much sleep during the night.

17.

    A. My anger does not make me feel any more tired than usual.

    B. My feelings of anger are beginning to tire me out.

    C. My anger is intense enough that it makes me feel very tired.

    D. My feelings of anger leave me too tired to do anything.

18.

    A. My appetite does not suffer because of my feelings of anger.

    B. My feelings of anger are beginning to affect my appetite.

    C. My feelings of anger leave me without much of an appetite.

    D. My anger is so intense that it has taken away my appetite.

19.

    A. My feelings of anger don't interfere with my health.

    B. My feelings of anger are beginning to interfere with my health.

    C. My anger prevents me from devoting much time and attention to my health.

    D. I'm so angry at everything these days that I pay no attention to my health and well-being.

20.

    A. My ability to think clearly is unaffected by my feelings of anger.

    B. Sometimes my feelings of anger prevent me from thinking in a clearheaded way.

    C. My anger makes it hard for me to think of anything else.

    D. I'm so intensely angry and hostile that it completely interferes with my thinking.

21. **A.** I don't feel so angry that it interferes with my interest in sex.

B. My feelings of anger leave me less interested in sex than I used to be.

C. My current feelings of anger undermine my interest in sex.

D. I'm so angry about my life that I've completely lost interest in sex.

For each A response that you chose, give yourself a score of 0 points. For each B response, score 1 point. For each C response, score 2 points. For each D response, score 3 points. Add up all your points to get your total score. As you might expect, a higher score indicates a higher level of anger.

0–13 points: Minimal clinical anger
- There is little to no significant anger.
- Proper sleep and nutrition are the best steps to take.

14–19 points: Mild clinical anger
- There are occasional brief feelings of anger.
- Relaxation techniques, exercise, and leisure activities are beneficial.

20–28 points: Moderate clinical anger
- There are intense or frequent feelings of anger.
- Short-term individual or group counseling can help in learning new coping skills.

29–63 points: Severe clinical anger
- There are frequent and intense feelings of anger.
- A lifestyle change is needed that involves psychological, medical, and relationship support.

SCORE   **NOTES**

Adapted from "The Clinical Anger Scale: Preliminary Reliability and Validity" (see Bibliography on page 149) and used with permission of Dr. William E. Snell Jr.

How Angry Are You?

Let's close with an exercise that helps you see for yourself how well you're coping now with anger so you can determine how problematic anger is for you in the present. Score yourself on the Clinical Anger Scale (page 38), and then answer the following questions.

What is the level of your anger?

_____

_____

_____

_____

_____

How do you feel about that assessment?

_____

_____

_____

_____

_____

On what symptoms of anger did you score highest?

_____

_____

_____

_____

_____

2 THE PHYSIOLOGY OF ANGER

DO YOU REMEMBER the Marvel Comics character known as Dr. Bruce Banner, that mild-mannered physicist who went from town to town doing good deeds? We all know what happened whenever he crossed paths with an antagonist—his face turned beet red, his eyes popped out, the vein in his forehead started throbbing, and he transformed into the green monster known as the Incredible Hulk. After the Hulk flipped a few cars, he'd revert to his former self and carry on.

The Hulk's transformation was pretty dramatic, but anyone who's chronically angry will also experience physical changes. That's because our bodies tell us what's important and what we need to attend to. For example, a growling stomach means that we need to eat, and a yawn often means that we need to sleep. If we ignore these messages from the body, then the body simply takes over, and we collapse from hunger or fatigue.

Anger is another kind of message from the body. It's the body's response to something it perceives as threatening. You may not even be consciously aware of the threat, but your body alerts you to the danger it perceives, and it does this so you can step in and take urgent action to neutralize the danger.

As we saw in chapter 1, the men who were our hunter-gatherer ancestors had to be constantly ready to size up a potential predator and then choose quickly between a fight to the death or a flight to safety. For them, there was no two ways about it—they would either live or die. But most situations in the modern world are far more nuanced, and they include contradictory elements—danger and safety, excitement and boredom, affection and irritation. That's why, in today's world, it's not always the big things that lead to eruptions of anger; sometimes it's the little things going on all the time—losing a parking space, getting stuck behind a slowpoke in the supermarket checkout line, stubbing your toe, a waiter dropping a tray of glasses that then shatter on the floor. These are the everyday stressors that overwhelm you and trigger your body's fight-or-flight response.

The moment your body perceives a threat, the brain undergoes striking changes. Communication breaks down between the prefrontal cortex, where rational thought and judgment reside, and the amygdala, where fear rules the day. Your brain gets pumped up on hormones like testosterone and noradrenalin and epinephrine. It's the latter two that pack the real emotional punch. But they also make you more focused and alert in response to the threat. You've probably experienced the surge of energy known as an *adrenaline rush*. This surge helps mobilize your muscles as it temporarily sharpens your senses and enhances certain types of memory.

Your rational mind is no match for your body's fight-or-flight response, and it will take you a full 20 minutes to calm down physically and psychologically even after the response has stopped.

As this automatic, instinctual response continues, your pupils dilate, your heart speeds up, your breathing becomes rapid and shallow, your digestion slows, and your perspiration increases. Your brain even becomes deprived of blood and oxygen as those precious resources are rushed directly to your large muscles so you'll be ready to move fast if you need to. You'll also be feeling especially sure of being in the right, and you'll be powerfully convinced that it's important for you to do something *right now*. And so it starts—the blaming, the arguing, the yelling, the hitting . . . the list goes on. After all, how can you think clearly when your brain is starving for blood and oxygen? Your rational mind is no match for your body's fight-or-flight response, and it will take you a full 20 minutes to calm down physically and psychologically even after the response has stopped.

There's nothing more urgent than danger, and as far as your body is concerned, you're back in the same neck of the woods where one of your ancient forebears was devoured by a predator capable of extinguishing the entire human species. Your fight-or-flight response tells you that you're facing a potentially fatal threat, that you must kill it or run away from it as fast as you can, and that you must not allow this threat to come anywhere near you ever again.

The fight-or-flight response is useful in the short term—it tells you that something is wrong, it opens your eyes to the situation around you, and it focuses your attention on what needs to be changed. But it's an emergency response, a state of high arousal that your body isn't built to maintain for very long. When this response endures over time, as it does when you're in a chronic state of anger, your body starts to break down. Then the same physiological changes that are meant to help you in an emergency start to disrupt your sleep and diminish your appetite. Instead of feeling energetic and mentally focused, you lose energy, and your judgment becomes impaired. Parts of your brain stop communicating with each other, and brain tissue shrinks in the regions that control learning, memory, and rational thought.

THE BRAIN'S DIVISION OF LABOR The prefrontal cortex and the amygdala have the same goal to help you survive—but they come at the task from different directions, and with different resources. The prefrontal cortex helps you reason your way through a problem. But when the amygdala perceives a threat to your survival, its hair-trigger emotional response overrules the sober judgment of the prefrontal cortex.

Coping and Working with Your Evolutionary Heritage

Our human ancestors developed the fight-or-flight response as a means of protection from predators. Modern people don't face the same kinds of danger, but that protective response lives on, although these days we usually experience it as anger.

What are some of the ways in which your anger serves to protect you?

_____
_____
_____
_____
_____
_____
_____
_____
_____
_____
_____
_____
_____
_____
_____
_____

Recognizing the Signs of Anger

When you're learning to manage your anger in a nonaggressive way, the first steps consist of recognizing how anger feels for you, and getting to know the situations that produce it. It's easier to take these first steps if you can become aware of your anger's characteristic physical, emotional, behavioral, and cognitive signs.

PHYSICAL SIGNS

Physical signs are often the first indications that you're becoming angry. If you can learn to recognize these signs as your responses to anger-provoking events, you can take steps to soothe yourself before your anger escalates to the point of losing control:

- Faster heart rate
- Higher blood pressure
- Increased sweating
- Muscle tightness
- Headache
- Trembling or twitching
- Nausea or vomiting
- Sleep problems
- Fatigue
- Shallow breathing

EMOTIONAL SIGNS

In chapter 1, we looked at how and why men suppress anger, and we talked about anger as a secondary emotion. Before you feel anger, you always have a different, primary feeling. It's often a feeling that causes you to see yourself as wrong or vulnerable in some way, but you may also just feel flat, apathetic, or depressed before you get angry. Getting angry may relieve that primary feeling, or it may continue alongside your anger. Either way, the discomfort of enduring primary feelings like these makes it easy for you to move quickly to anger:

- Hostility
- Sadness
- Guilt
- Jealousy
- Shock
- Worry
- Defensiveness
- Suspiciousness
- Shame
- Apathy (lack of interest)
- Panic
- Pessimism

BEHAVIORAL SIGNS

Behavioral signs of anger involve your tone of voice, posture, and other kinds of body language as well as direct and indirect actions like these:

- Clenching your fists
- Pacing back and forth
- Slamming a door
- Kicking or throwing something
- Getting in someone's face
- Shoving, grabbing, or hitting
- Breaking something
- Calling someone names

- Giving someone a dirty look
- Giving someone the silent treatment
- Committing acts of road rage
- Drinking or using drugs
- Eating too much or too little
- Blaming others
- Making accusations
- Yelling

REALITY, IMAGINATION, AND THE BRAIN

Your brain has no way of knowing whether you're watching *Mad Max: Fury Road* or viewing real-life events. Your prefrontal cortex tells you that you're watching sequences of still images projected at a rate of 24 frames per second. Meanwhile, your amygdala gets your heart pounding as the War Boys chase Max Rockatansky across a post-apocalyptic Australian landscape.

If your brain can't tell the difference between what's dangerous and what isn't, then everything is a potential threat, and you're in for a lot of false alarms. For example, your prefrontal cortex is responsible for remembering that your ex-wife is a petite brunette who dumped you. Your amygdala is in charge of flooding your body with rage whenever you see a woman who even vaguely resembles her. And *vaguely* is the operative word here, since the amygdala, in its effort to determine whether that petite brunette in the coffee shop presents a clear and present danger, rapidly evaluates her against your store of emotionally charged memories. The amygdala's motto is "Better safe than sorry," and so if it finds any key similarity at all—a tone of voice, a facial expression—it instantly activates its warning siren and sets off an emotional explosion in your body. So if you've ever wondered why anger has a way of stirring up memories of long-ago threats and painful events, now you know.

COGNITIVE SIGNS

Cognitive signs have to do with the thoughts you have in response to an anger-provoking event. When you're angry, you may think that a friend's neutral comments are critical of you, or you may think that others' actions are demeaning, humiliating, or controlling. Some people call thoughts like these *negative self-talk* because they're like a conversation you're having with yourself about the world and other people. Closely related to this kind of self-talk are vengeful fantasies of defeating a perceived enemy and painful images of betrayal by someone you love. Thoughts, self-talk, fantasies, and images like these can make your anger escalate very rapidly, and they're almost always focused on other people. But taking the focus off yourself puts control of an anger-provoking situation in someone else's hands. You can learn to take negative self-talk as an indication of rising tension within yourself. If you notice yourself having thoughts like the ones listed below, try to remember that changing your tone or behavior can prevent an unnecessarily negative interaction with someone else:

- He did that on purpose.
- She wanted to hurt me.
- You deserved this.
- They never even asked me.
- She's being unreasonable.
- They think they're better than me.
- I'll show him.
- It's not fair!
- He started it.
- She doesn't care about me.
- They can't be trusted.

Tuning In to Your Anger

For you, what are the principal physical signs of anger?
Do you notice different physical signs in different situations
or with different people in your life?

_____

_____

_____

_____

_____

_____

_____

_____

_____

For you, what are the principal emotional signs of anger? Are you aware
of any primary feelings that are typically behind your anger?

_____

_____

_____

_____

_____

_____

_____

_____

_____

For you, what are the principal behavioral signs of anger?

_____

_____

_____

_____

_____

_____

_____

_____

_____

_____

Is your angry behavior typically more direct and active (slamming a door, throwing something) or more indirect and passive (clenching your fists, using a particular tone of voice)?

_____

_____

_____

_____

_____

_____

_____

_____

_____

Do you express anger directly in some situations and indirectly in others?

_____

_____

_____

_____

_____

_____

_____

_____

Do you ever engage in angry behavior that primarily hurts yourself (overeating, drinking too much, using drugs)?

_____

_____

_____

_____

_____

_____

_____

_____

_____

For you, what are the principal cognitive signs of anger?

_____

_____

_____

_____

_____

_____

_____

_____

If you have fantasies of revenge, or if you imagine being betrayed by a friend or a loved one, how do you feel physically as these events play out in your mind?

_____

_____

_____

_____

_____

_____

_____

_____

Learning to Relax

If you're stressed out and chronically angry, the logical, natural antidote to your stressful state is relaxation. After all, you can't be enraged and relaxed at the same time—it's physiologically impossible. Relaxation is always within your reach because all it requires you to do is the things you do anyway: sleep, eat, and breathe. You just need to train yourself to do these things in a different way.

SLEEPING SOUNDLY

If you're not getting enough sleep, or if the quality of your sleep is poor, then you're more likely to feel irritable, angry, and hostile, and you'll react more intensely to small, ordinary frustrations and disappointments. That's because insomnia and poor sleep are associated with higher activity in the amygdala (more anger) and reduced functioning in the prefrontal cortex of your brain (poorer judgment). Here are a few tips to improve the quality of your sleep:

- **Do not nap during the day.** If you nap in the daytime, you disrupt your internal clock and make it even more difficult to fall asleep at night. If you're especially tired and feel that you absolutely must nap, do it early in the day, and set an alarm so you don't sleep for more than 30 minutes.
- **Limit your intake of caffeine and alcohol.** Cut yourself off from these beverages several hours before bedtime. Alcohol may cause you to feel drowsy at first, but it can interrupt your sleep later on during the night and can contribute to a disrupted sleep pattern.
- **Don't smoke.** Nicotine is a stimulant. If you smoke, you may find it hard to fall asleep and stay asleep.
- **Keep your bedroom peaceful and comfortable.** Your room should be well ventilated, and the temperature should be consistent. Try to keep your bedroom quiet, too. A fan or a white-noise machine can help block outside noises.
- **Hide your clock.** Put your clock in a spot that you can't see from your bed. When you're trying to fall asleep, the last thing you need is a big illuminated digital clock inviting you to focus on the time and feel stressed and anxious.

DOES ANGER CAUSE ILLNESS?

To say that anger causes illness would be to overstate what anger can do. But we know that anger brings about a state of high physiological arousal, and that chronic anger takes a toll on the body. Here are some health problems in which unmanaged anger can play a role, either in the short term or over the long run:

- Headaches
- Digestive problems, such as abdominal pain
- Insomnia
- Mental health problems, such as excessive anxiety and depression
- Skin problems, such as eczema
- Cardiovascular problems, such as heart attacks, strokes, and high blood pressure

EATING WELL

As you know by now, when you ignore an important signal from your body, your body reacts in a way that's intended to grab your attention, and the longer you ignore your body's signal, the stronger your body's reaction will be. So here's a word you should know: *hanger*. It's not just a word for the familiar object that lives in your closet. It's also a word for the anger that a 2012 *Biological Psychiatry* article says you're likely to feel if you go too long without eating and let yourself get too hungry. Here are some tips for keeping "hanger" at bay:

- **Always make sure you have some healthy food with you.** Trying to soothe "hanger" with candy or other types of junk food will just create a vicious cycle as your blood sugar shoots sky-high for 30 minutes and then crashes, leaving you even hungrier (and angrier) than before.
- **Don't skip meals.** Missing a meal means missing an opportunity to provide your mind and body with energy. You shouldn't go more than four to five hours between meals. If you prefer not to snack between meals, consider having five small meals spaced throughout the day instead of the typical breakfast, lunch, and dinner.

- **Snack smart.** If you do choose to snack between meals, use the tried-and-true trio of protein, fat, and carbohydrates to keep yourself going without blowing a fuse. A slice of cheese and a few whole-grain crackers, an apple and a handful of trail mix, celery sticks spread with peanut butter, or other on-the-go snacks can come to your rescue when you feel your mood diving and an emotional meltdown coming on.

BREATHING DEEPLY

Remember what people have told you about taking a deep breath as soon as you feel upset? It may be a cliché, but it's still good advice. That's because your first reaction to frustration or other kinds of emotional upset is purely physiological—you experience a rush of adrenaline that prepares you to take action in the face of danger. Just taking a few moments to breathe deeply is usually all it takes to calm your body down. When you deliberately take slow, deep breaths, you tell your body that all danger has passed, and your body stops producing adrenaline. Slow, deep breathing slows your heart down, lowers your blood pressure, and releases endorphins, your body's natural stress relievers.

Breathe Your Way to Relaxation

Place your hand on your chest. Breathe in and out through your mouth in big sighs so that you feel your chest moving toward and away from your hand. This is *chest breathing*, a shallow form of respiration that is often a response to stress. Rapid chest breathing quickly gets oxygen to your muscles so you can fight if you need to, or run away from whatever is stressing you. Your heart rate and your blood pressure rise, and you feel revved up. If at any point you feel dizzy or lightheaded, slow your breathing down. But continue to breathe this way for one minute, noting how you feel at the end of that time.

Place your hand on your stomach, just below your ribs. Begin by breathing in slowly and deeply through your nose, as if you were smelling a fragrant flower, and as you inhale, silently say the word *in*. Pucker your lips and breathe out, slowly and gradually, as if you were blowing at a candle just enough to make the flame flicker, and as you exhale, silently say the word *out* and feel your stomach moving up and down under your hand. Don't force it—just breathe in and out, quietly and evenly, at your own pace. Bring your attention to the way the air feels as it passes through your nostrils on the way in, and as it streams out over your lips on the way out. This is *abdominal breathing*, the deep, natural way you breathed as a baby and still breathe when you're asleep or very calm. Continue to breathe this way for one minute, and note how you feel at the end of that time.

Now compare how you felt physically after one minute of chest breathing and how you felt physically after one minute of abdominal breathing.

Were there any differences in the way your heart was beating after you performed each type of breathing?

_____

_____

_____

_____

Was your emotional state any different with the two types of breathing? What about your thoughts?

_____

_____

_____

_____

_____

Try deep breathing the next time you experience a tension headache, a backache, insomnia, or some other physical manifestation of stress. It's also a good idea to set aside some time every day to do deep breathing. Start by practicing while you're lying in bed and ready for sleep.

If you can do deep breathing when you're not feeling angry, then it will be easier for you to use deep breathing as a remedy in times of stress. And as you become more adept, you may find yourself moving automatically into deep-breathing mode whenever stress arises.

> _You can deepen your state of relaxation if you imagine breathing in the freshness of ocean air, a favorite perfume, the smell of roasting coffee, the aroma of cookies baking in the oven, or any other scent that you associate with comfort and pleasure._

PART 2

MANAGING ANGER

3 MIND OVER ANGER

An old man was teaching his grandson about life.

"A fierce fight is going on inside me," the man said to the boy. "It is between two wolves. One wolf is evil. He is guilt, anger, envy, regret, greed, arrogance, self-pity, resentment, lies, inferiority, false pride, superiority, self-doubt, and ego. The second wolf is good. He is joy, peace, love, hope, serenity, humility, kindness, benevolence, empathy, generosity, truth, compassion, and faith. It is a terrible fight, and the same fight is going on inside you, and inside every other person, too."

The boy thought for a minute about what his grandfather had said.

"Which wolf will win the fight?" the boy asked.

The old man replied simply, "The one that I feed."

ANGER IS AN automatic physiological response, like blinking or breathing. Just as you can decide to take conscious control over when and how you blink and breathe, you can take control of the angry thoughts that produce your automatic response of anger.

This chapter explores how and where you learned to cope with anger, and how different kinds of unhelpful advice may have shaped your responses to anger-provoking events. The chapter also looks at how outbursts of aggression can be triggered by interpretations of people and events. In addition, the chapter discusses some healing techniques for letting go of anger.

Anger as Learned Behavior

Human beings learn by mirroring other humans, even on the first day of life—stick your tongue out at a newborn, and the infant is likely to stick its tongue out at you in response. This means that imitation laid the groundwork for everything you have ever learned. What it also means is that when you were a child and someone used a nasty tone with you, you probably learned to use that tone yourself. Or if one of your parents left the room whenever you got angry, you may have learned to respond that way to other people's anger—regardless of how rejected, isolated, and abandoned your own parent's response might have made you feel. Like many other men, you may not remember being taught how to cope with your own and others' anger, but those lessons did take place, and you learned them either directly or indirectly through observation.

In general, people get angry because they want something or someone to change, but they can't figure out how to make it happen. In this situation, a feeling of powerlessness arises, along with the desire to not feel or appear powerless.

An angry man who feels powerless is anxious about disclosing his vulnerability. As a result, he also feels insecure because the situation all but invites him to compare himself to others and then feel inferior to those supposedly smarter and more competent people. His anger builds, and he begins to resent those people for their superior coping skills, and to hate himself for being so stupid.

As this process continues, he turns to the problematic emotional lessons he learned in childhood. He may also turn to friends or family members for advice that turns out to be anything but helpful and only makes him angrier. From there, it's just a short step to concluding that there must be something wrong with him for feeling the way he does and being the way he is. In short, nothing he's ever learned or heard about anger turns out to be helpful when he's actually angry.

PROBLEMATIC EMOTIONAL LESSONS

When you can identify the lessons you were taught about emotions and the ways they should be handled, you become more capable of changing how you experience and express anger. Here are some lessons you may have learned in childhood:

- Always treat other people's feelings as more important than your own.
- Never do anything that might make someone else unhappy.
- Don't express anger.
- Getting angry gets attention.
- Ignore your feelings—or, better still, don't even have feelings.
- Don't trust others with your feelings—keep your feelings to yourself.
- Never trust your feelings—trust only logic.
- Be happy all the time.
- Men don't cry.

What emotional lessons were you taught?

_____

_____

_____

_____

_____

_____

_____

_____

_____

_____

_____

Seeing Through Useless Advice

Much of the anger-management advice that people think is helpful actually makes things worse. It leaves the recipient feeling angry because he senses that he's not really being seen or understood. And, needless to say, it doesn't solve the problem.

Each of the following examples of useless advice is accompanied by one or more comments on the nature of the advice or its likely effects. After each example, write a few words about a situation in which the advice was offered to you, and answer the following questions:

How did you react? What else can you say about the effect the advice had on your struggle with anger?

"You have only yourself to blame." This remark not only focuses on who is to blame, it blames the victim—you—because it accuses you of causing the problem and then failing to solve it. Instead of helping you understand the problem, it encourages you to feel inadequate, incompetent, and inferior.

_____

_____

_____

_____

_____

_____

_____

_____

_____

"You don't want to change—you like being in pain." This is another instance of advice that blames the victim. Would-be helpers say this when they feel inadequate to solve a problem. It's true that some people do use their pain and suffering to manipulate others and gain what that they feel they can't obtain in a healthier way. Maybe you've done this yourself. But the larger truth is that people don't enjoy their suffering, and no one likes to be in pain.

_____

_____

_____

_____

_____

_____

_____

_____

"Getting angry doesn't do any good." This is a true statement. As advice, however, it's on a par with saying, "There's no use coming down with chicken pox." The fact is that men get angry whether it does any good or not. Rather than state the obvious, it would be better for your would-be helper to ask you, "How can you manage your anger in a way that brings you the relief you need and doesn't cause you any more pain?"

_____

_____

_____

_____

_____

_____

_____

"No one can make you angry without your permission." This is another example of blaming the victim. You're not made of stone. You can learn to respect yourself no matter how others behave, and you don't have to imitate or return their ill treatment or bad behavior. But the would-be helper who dispenses this advice is essentially telling you that anger is never legitimate.

_____

_____

_____

_____

_____

_____

_____

_____

"Be nice, or else no one will like you." The message here is to value niceness above all else. But the world isn't always nice, and this piece of advice is a setup for the recipient to internalize anger and blow a gasket later on instead of managing anger in the present, in a healthy way.

_____

_____

_____

_____

_____

_____

_____

_____

"What will people think?" This isn't really a question. It is advice—very strong advice presented as an order. The order is "Shut up," and the person, who responds this way when you get angry in public, often someone close to you, is telling you that the approval of anonymous passersby is more important than a loved one's distress.

_____

_____

_____

_____

_____

_____

_____

_____

_____

"You can solve any problem if you just put your mind to it." This advice is consistent with exaggerated male ideals of independence and pragmatism. But just as some problems of the heart won't show up on an EKG, not every problem you face can be solved with your head—that is, rationally.

_____

_____

_____

_____

_____

_____

_____

_____

_____

"It's all good." No, it isn't. But many men are much more comfortable pretending that it is, than they are dealing with what isn't so good, and they'll be relieved if you adopt that stance, too.

_____

_____

_____

_____

_____

_____

_____

_____

_____

_____

"It's nothing to worry about." This is the advice you get when your would-be helper can't solve the problem and hopes it goes away.

_____

_____

_____

_____

_____

_____

_____

_____

_____

_____

"Stop thinking about it. There's nothing you can do." This is another piece of advice that people give you when they feel unable to offer a solution. But the past is not dead. Your emotional pain is alive and affects you in the present. You can't make things better in the present by deciding not to think about painful events in your past.

_____

_____

_____

_____

_____

_____

_____

"You have no right to be upset." The person who makes this pronouncement is advising you to put an emotional issue inside a rational frame. It's true that there are more and less appropriate ways to *express* anger, but your right to *feel* anger is never in question. When anger becomes an emotional problem, it responds to emotional solutions, not to rationalistic prohibitions. But this remark isn't very rational anyway, since it basically amounts to shaming you for being angry.

_____

_____

_____

_____

_____

_____

_____

Advice is like cooking—you should taste what you're dishing out before you feed it to others.

UNHELPFUL ADVICE

Wherever you turn, it seems there's someone waiting to give you advice. People have built whole careers on telling men how to be caring fathers, loving husbands, and good providers. And you don't even have to see a professional adviser—your friends and family members, with every good intention, are more than happy to weigh in when they see that you're in distress.

Unfortunately, however, when it comes to unmanaged anger, most people are not experts, and so they don't really know how to address the problem. They may be able to tell you about solutions that worked for them, but their solutions may not work for you. Or, because they really want to help, they'll parrot received wisdom like "Change yourself, and everything else will change." That kind of advice prescribes a goal but tells you nothing at all about how to reach it.

People give advice for all kinds of reasons, often because they mean well and really want to help. But wanting to help is not the same as actually being able to help. When you find yourself on the receiving end of advice from would-be helpers, acknowledge their kind intentions, but feel free to disengage from any obligation to follow their suggestions.

DOES MANAGING ANGER MEAN PREVENTING DISASTER?

You may have come to believe that managing anger means being able to prevent other people from hurting you, or having the power to ward off other kinds of personal disaster. If that's what you believe, then you also have to believe that you can see the future, and that you can solve problems before they arise.

But when you buy the idea that managing anger means preventing disaster, you set yourself up to feel inadequate. You can't possibly predict the future with perfect accuracy, and so when disaster strikes in spite of your belief that you could have prevented it, you blame yourself for not having seen it coming.

What connections can you make between your anger and the belief that managing anger means preventing bad things from happening?

_____

_____

_____

_____

_____

What You See Is What You Get

Once when I was watching the news, I saw a story about a man in southern California whose house had been destroyed by a mudslide. He was crying, and he told a reporter that he wanted the federal government to step in and help. Down the street, the reporter found another man who had suffered the same fate. "My family got out all right," this man told her. "All our stuff is buried in the mud, but we can save a lot of it." When she asked him what would come next for him and his family, the man said, "I've always wanted a third bedroom." The first man looked at his ruined house and saw nothing but loss. The second man saw the opportunity to save what he could of his past and then go on to build a better future. The first man saw loss, and what he got was helpless sorrow. The second man saw possibility, and what he got was hopeful energy.

In other words, how you interpret a situation determines what you will feel about it. By the same token, what you've felt about a situation in the past will influence the way you interpret a similar situation in the future, even though the similarity may be slight. For example, if you've become hypersensitive to signals of rejection, then you may feel snubbed by something as random and meaningless as two strangers at your bus stop having a conversation that doesn't include you. And, as you might expect, if you're frequently angry, then you may tend to interpret neutral events in anger-provoking ways.

CONFIRMATION BIAS Your brain is adept at detecting a whole pattern from just a few clues. One result is that you're susceptible to confirmation bias, a type of selective thinking that causes you to notice evidence for what you already believe, and to miss or discount evidence that might lead in another direction. When life unfailingly conforms to your most negative expectations, you can be sure that confirmation bias is at work.

When you feel anger or any other emotion, your feeling is the product of two factors:

1 The objective physiological arousal that a particular event produces in you
2 Your subjective interpretation of the event

For example, when someone steps on your toe, you feel pain, and your heart starts to beat faster. These automatic reactions are your body's initial physical response to the event. If you interpret this event as an accident, you'll still be in physical pain, but you won't be angry. But if you interpret the event as a deliberate provocation, you'll probably react with anger. The physiological arousal caused by an event is involuntary, but you have a choice about how you interpret the event, which means that you also have a choice about your emotional reaction. It's your interpretation, not the event itself, that is the key to your emotional experience. If you find that you're often in a state of anger, you may want to examine the interpretations you're bringing to events, since your interpretations may be promoting angry thoughts that color your expectations about how your life will unfold.

Arousal + Interpretation = Emotion

Challenging Your Angry Thoughts

Distorted thinking involves thoughts that flash into your mind and make you feel worse. When you're angry, take a look at your thoughts. Are you making errors in how you interpret situations? Look for recurring patterns like the ones described below.

Taking things personally. You look for and expect criticism from other people, and when you find it, you feel hurt. But sometimes things just aren't about you. A cranky person who snaps at you may simply be having a bad day and not handling his or her own anger very well.

Do you sometimes take things personally, even when they have little or nothing to do with you, and then feel hurt or angry? List a few examples.

_____

_____

_____

_____

_____

_____

_____

_____

_____

_____

_____

_____

_____

Ignoring the positive. You focus on the negative aspects of a situation and ignore the positive ones. For example, you're given many compliments, but you fixate instead on a single piece of negative feedback.

Do you sometimes ignore the positive aspects of situations? List a few examples.

_____

_____

_____

_____

_____

_____

_____

Seeking perfection. You expect too much from yourself and those around you. When others don't meet your high standards, you feel disappointed and hurt, and your hurt quickly turns to anger. When perfectionism reigns, it's often impossible for you to see that others are consistently supportive of you even though they're not flawless.

Do you sometimes expect perfection from yourself or others? List a few examples.

_____

_____

_____

_____

_____

_____

_____

Seeing situations as unfair. There is no absolute standard when it comes to how people think about what's fair and unfair. To say that something is fair or unfair is to make a subjective judgment on the basis of what you want, need, or expect from a particular situation.

Do you sometimes encounter unfairness? List a few examples.

_____

_____

_____

_____

_____

_____

Making self-fulfilling prophecies. On the basis of a single unpleasant event, you draw pessimistic, cynical, and defeatist conclusions about life as a whole. You see the world through the prism of your negative thoughts and expect the worst. That's often what you get, too.

Do you sometimes jump to negative conclusions and then see and experience the world through them? List a few examples.

_____

_____

_____

_____

_____

_____

Thinking in all-or-nothing terms. Black-and-white thinking takes you out of the middle ground where most of real life happens. For example, you feel betrayed when a good friend disappoints you—maybe because you were uncomfortable telling him what you wanted and expected in a particular situation—and the next time you see him, you angrily tell him you'll never trust him again.

Do you sometimes think in black-and-white, all-or-nothing terms? List a few examples.

_____

_____

_____

_____

_____

_____

_____

To manage your anger, it's important to recognize and challenge distorted patterns of thinking like these. Here are four steps for spotting where your thinking may be going wrong.

1. **Describe a situation in which you might easily become angry (for example, someone cuts in front of you in the line at the post office).**

_____

_____

_____

_____

_____

_____

2. Write down what makes you angry about this situation (for example, cutting in line is inconsiderate to everyone else).

_____

_____

_____

_____

_____

3. Notice your self-talk, and write it down (for example, "People nowadays are so rude").

_____

_____

_____

_____

_____

4. Ask yourself if it would really make any difference if the situation you described were to play out in real life.

_____

_____

_____

_____

_____

Most of the time, situations like the one you just described don't amount to a hill of beans, and so it makes no sense for you to lash out. But it's quite reasonable for you to feel angry about things you don't like, and you can use your anger constructively if you let it energize you to change situations you're unhappy with. In this way, you can choose to see anger as being neither good nor bad—just human.

How Thoughts Shape Responses: A Clinical Example

Gabriel had been married to Nancy for 12 years. He would fly into uncontrollable rages over nothing at all, and when Nancy asked him why, he would always say, "I don't know what got into me." By the time Gabriel sought professional help, Nancy was afraid of his anger and was even afraid that just talking to him might be enough to set off an eruption. She was anxious most of the time when he was home, and sometimes even when he wasn't. Here's how one of Gabriel's sessions with his therapist unfolded:

Therapist: What made you so angry last week when Nancy asked you to help with the housework?

Gabriel: It was the way she said it.

Therapist: What way was that?

Gabriel: Telling me what to do. Not giving me a choice. It sounded like an order—do it now, or else. I hate that.

Therapist: Who does that remind you of?

Gabriel: My father. She sounds just like him when she gets like that.

Therapist: What did your father do when you didn't do what he wanted?

Gabriel: He'd yell and threaten to punish me if I didn't do it fast enough or if I didn't do it right.

Therapist: What did "doing it right" mean to you?

Gabriel: It meant doing it his way, or else.

Therapist: Did you know what his way was?

Gabriel: I thought I did, but he'd always find something wrong.

Therapist: What is it called when there isn't anything wrong at all?

Gabriel: That never happened.

Therapist: It's called *perfection*, and no human is perfect. It wasn't fair that you were required to be perfect. And as a child, you couldn't figure out what was a mistake and what wasn't. If you can't tell what is a mistake, how can you correct it? You couldn't read his mind. He set you up to be criticized and punished. Did you ever feel that no matter what you did, it wasn't good enough to get his approval?

Gabriel: I still feel that way with Nancy.

Therapist: Your emotional memory doesn't know the difference. It feels the same way. Your heart doesn't have eyes and can't tell someone from the past from someone in the present. It wasn't helpful that your father blamed you for not meeting his unrealistic expectations, but it isn't helpful for you to lash out at Nancy, either. That is what your father did to you. It never made you feel better, and it's making her feel the pain now that you felt then.

Gabriel: I never thought of it that way before.

Therapist: Do you think you can catch yourself living in the past and choose to live in the present?

Gabriel: I never knew I had a choice.

Therapist: Your father is an imperfect human who expressed his painful self-contempt by dumping criticism on you. That wasn't fair. How can anyone criticize a person, a child, for being imperfect, as if it were the child's fault? No human is perfect, nor can you be expected to be. It wasn't fair—you couldn't win. It was only a matter of time before you got yelled at and punished. Did this unfairness make you angry?

Gabriel: Yes.

Therapist: Who are you angry at?

Gabriel: At him, for yelling and blaming me. I only wanted to please him and make him happy, but I never could.

Therapist: You took his behavior personally. He made you feel like a failure as a son and a human. Who else are you angry at?

Gabriel: I'm angry at myself for being such a screw-up. I kept trying, and I was never good enough to please him. But why would I keep trying if I knew I would fail? I must be an idiot.

Therapist: You are ignoring your efforts. You're blaming yourself for outcomes that you can't control. When did you get over it?

Gabriel: Get over it? I'm still living it right now!

Therapist: You have a choice about whether or not you want to keep holding on to this anger at past circumstances. This pent-up emotion has already begun to leak into your marriage, and it will kill your happiness. Nancy wants to know why you can't cooperate with her and help around the house. She's afraid to ask you for anything.

Gabriel: I don't blame her. I didn't even know she was scared of me. I don't want that. I just get too wrapped up in myself to consider her feelings.

Therapist: Well, you learned that. No one ever considered *your* feelings. Feelings were not valued in your family. Neither was cooperation. Your father didn't try to cooperate. He sought your submission. And he taught you how to lash out and seek submission to achieve your own definition of perfection. This is an example of negative control.

Gabriel: When Nancy tells me to do something, all those old feelings come back to me. I feel like I'm being forced—like I have no choice. I feel like a victim. Like I'm going to get punished for not doing it the right way.

Therapist: You feel controlled by her.

Gabriel: I *am* controlled by her.

Therapist: Feeling out of control is painful. And you want to relieve this pain as fast as you can.

Gabriel: Wouldn't you?

Therapist: Is your way working? Does it give you relief? Or are you left in even more pain because of the guilt you feel after acting in ways that are even more out of control?

Gabriel: I never thought of it that way. I do feel more out of control, but I don't know what else to do.

Therapist: Can you choose to ask Nancy if it really has to be done right away, or if it can wait a few minutes until you're ready?

Gabriel: That's hard for me.

Therapist: What's the hardest thing about it?

Gabriel: It's like I'm asking permission.

Therapist: Do you have the right to ask for what you want?

Gabriel: Yes.

Therapist: On what basis?

Gabriel: I don't know.

Therapist: As an equal member of the human race. Not superior or inferior, better or worse. You and Nancy and your father are unconditionally lovable and worthwhile, despite your mistakes and imperfections. You don't have to prove your worth or defend yourself from others' judgments. You get to be the judge, and you get to determine how good is good enough to feel like a success.

Gabriel: I never thought about it like that. I'm always trying to do everything by myself, but no matter how hard I tried, I never could.

Therapist: It must be very frustrating and discouraging. You can outgrow this learning from your childhood by pushing your comfort zone and asking Nancy for what you want. It's not begging. It's a request for cooperation between two equal members of the human race.

Gabriel: What if I don't get what I'm asking for?

Therapist: Will it make you angry?

Gabriel: Yes.

Therapist: Will you take it personally?

Gabriel: Yes. I'll feel like an idiot—like I should have known better.

Therapist: You won't be an idiot. Do you define your self-worth in terms of Nancy's approval? You can't always please everyone. You can't read other people's minds. You don't really know what pleases them. You have enough trouble figuring out what pleases you! You can catch yourself when you're about to react to Nancy in the old way, out of fear of being punished for failing and displeasing her. Instead you can choose to live in the present. You can listen to what she's actually saying, not what you feel like she's saying. She's not your father. She's your imperfect wife, in the present. She's not superior, you're not inferior, and you're both equal members of the human race.

Gabriel: How do I remember that?

Therapist: By pushing your comfort zone and asking Nancy for her cooperation, as one adult to another. You can say, "Nancy, is it all right if I do the dishes after the kids go to bed? I don't get to see them that much these days." Can you do that?

Gabriel: I don't know.

Therapist: There's one way to find out, and that is to push out of your comfort zone and take the risk when the opportunity arises. Who is in control of your choice?

Gabriel: I guess I am.

Therapist: If you don't, who will? It's up to you—you're all you've got control over.

A major insight for Gabriel was that cooperation is not submission, and that trying to please someone else—his father years before, or his wife in the present—is not the way to be in control, and not the way to prevent disaster (as if that were even possible). Instead, as Gabriel was beginning to learn, trying to control a situation by living up to someone else's standards is bound to engender feelings of guilt that can eventually lead to out-of-control anger.

Techniques for Letting Go of Anger

In this section, we'll look at three powerful ways to speed up the process of healing from anger: practicing forgiveness of others' hurtful behavior, nurturing self-respect, and writing about situations that provoke anger and other painful emotions.

PRACTICING FORGIVENESS

When you hold on to past hurt, you're actually trying to relieve your pain by putting other people down and building yourself up. You may imagine that nursing old wounds is the way to be in control and prevent the humiliating exposure of your imperfections. You may even entertain vengeful fantasies of finally achieving fairness by hurting the people who hurt you. But instead of trying to control or redeem a hurtful situation, you can focus on managing your reaction to it.

One of the best ways to heal from anger is to forgive the people who hurt you. The act of forgiveness gives you new options for living your life on a much more realistic basis. Besides, if you don't forgive old wounds, they'll stay deep down inside you forever. Is that what you want?

Forgiveness has nothing to do with condoning or excusing the wrongs that were done to you. It means letting go of those old wounds so you can move on with your life. And forgiveness has nothing to do with assessing the degree of other people's guilt, or the relative evil of their intentions. That's because forgiveness is not about other people at all.

You forgive others for your own benefit, not theirs. The people who hurt you don't even have to know that you've forgiven their hurtful behavior. Your act of forgiveness is between you and yourself—it's no one else's business. In chapter 4, we'll look at some ways to foster forgiveness by not taking others' wounding behavior personally.

NURTURING SELF-RESPECT

When you're angry or facing antagonism from someone else, your most important resource is your self-respect. To respect yourself is to know that you are a worthwhile human being in spite of your mistakes. You may be at fault in a situation, but you're a human being. Human beings are not perfect, and perfection should never be expected of a human being.

You can respect yourself regardless of what's going on in your life. That's because self-respect doesn't depend on getting what you want—a promotion at work, the ideal mate, a higher income—or on your ability to be perfect. Respecting yourself means accepting that you are unconditionally lovable, no matter what anyone else says.

All men make mistakes. Self-respecting men learn from theirs. You should learn from yours, too, because you can't prevent them. You can take reasonable precautions, but past that point, your efforts at prevention become counterproductive—you exercise no control over things that have yet to happen, and trying to read others' minds so you can know what they want from you is not going to keep you from disappointing them at times.

> *When you tell someone you're sorry, you're not admitting guilt. You're expressing regret that you're not perfect. Human imperfection is regrettable, but you're never on trial for being human.*

WRITING

When I think about the power of writing, I'm reminded of a former client. John had served in Iraq, and he looked as if he'd also put in time with the Hells Angels.

John didn't come to me voluntarily. During his hearing on a drunk-driving offense, he was ordered into counseling for anger management after he took exception to something the judge said and charged the bench, breaking two of his own ribs in the process.

At our first session, John blamed both his angry outburst and his broken ribs on the judge, who had enraged him even more by ordering him to seek treatment. I suggested to John that he write about how he was feeling.

> **The process of uncovering painful memories is like peeling an onion—it may stink and make you cry, but it's how you get to what heals you.**

"No way," John snapped. "It's not going to work, and I don't have time anyway."

"Well," I told him, "you have a choice. What you're doing to manage your anger isn't working for you, but you can keep doing that and hope for a different outcome. Or you can try writing."

I gave him a legal pad and set up an appointment for the following week.

When John returned, he handed me the pad. "Here you go, doc."

I flipped through the pages. Every one was covered with John's random, scrawled expletives. Keeping a straight face, I asked him how the writing had made him feel.

John finally cracked a smile.

"A little better, actually," he admitted. "I haven't been as tense."

I handed him another pad.

"Keep writing," I said.

Keeping a Journal

Writing about your experiences may seem counterintuitive—you may wish to forget your distress and pain—but keeping a journal can help you release painful emotions and see things more objectively, without attachment to feelings from the past. Writing also helps you gain insight into how your angry thoughts affect your interpretations of events, and gives you control over how and when your feelings come to the surface, as they inevitably will. When you keep your thoughts abstract, locked up in your mind, you can't evaluate how well they reflect your actual life or yourself as you really are. But when your thoughts are right in front of you, in black and white, you can begin to sort them out.

To evaluate your angry feelings in a practical way, begin by answering these questions:

What situation are you writing about?

_____
_____
_____
_____
_____
_____

What is the worst thing about this situation?

_____
_____
_____
_____
_____
_____

How does this situation make you feel?

_____

_____

_____

_____

_____

_____

When else have you felt this way?

_____

_____

_____

_____

_____

_____

After answering the questions, go back to the first one, and repeat the process. Go through the questions until you uncover some seemingly unrelated memory or experience. The process of uncovering painful memories is like peeling an onion—it may stink and make you cry, but it's how you get to what heals you.

You can also write about your anger in the form of a letter to the person who hurt or offended you. At the time, your feelings about the situation may have been unconscious or unacceptable to you. But when you bring those feelings into your awareness and make them concrete, you can move forward as you resolve the conflict between your conscious, rational mind and your conscious or unconscious emotional reactions.

To make the most of your writing, develop some habits:

Set aside a regular time for writing. Opening your journal as soon as you get up in the morning is good for remembering dreams as well as for planning. Writing in your journal just before you go to sleep is good for reviewing the day.

Associate writing with a particular spot. That spot may be your desk, a comfortable chair, or even a public place like a park, a café, or the food court at a shopping mall.

Use props, such as a favorite pen or a special notebook. You may find that just the act of picking up your pen or notebook starts the juices flowing.

When you write what's on your mind and in your heart, you affirm not only your ability to manage your anger but also the validity of your feelings. You confirm your sense of self and give legitimacy to your existence *as* yourself—not as a son, brother, husband, friend, or employee—in the real world, in real time, not in your dreams, your imagination, or your fantasies. You're in control—acting, not reacting.

Here are some more questions you can use to get your thoughts and memories flowing:

In the situation you're writing about, what were you trying to achieve?

_____

_____

_____

_____

_____

_____

If you had achieved what you wanted, how would that have affected your life in the long term?

_____

_____

_____

_____

_____

_____

_____

What would have been the ideal outcome of the situation?

_____

_____

_____

_____

_____

_____

_____

What advice would you give to someone else in the same situation?

_____

_____

_____

_____

_____

_____

_____

What was it about the situation that angered you the most?

_____
_____
_____
_____
_____
_____
_____

Who were you most angry with?

_____
_____
_____
_____
_____
_____

How else did you feel?

_____
_____
_____
_____
_____
_____

How did the situation develop?

_____
_____
_____
_____
_____
_____

What was going through your mind as the situation unfolded?

_____
_____
_____
_____
_____
_____

What was going on in your life at the time?

_____
_____
_____
_____
_____
_____

How do you feel now just thinking about the situation?

_____

_____

_____

_____

_____

_____

Does the situation remind you of anyone other than the people who were involved in it?

_____

_____

_____

_____

_____

_____

_____

What did you learn from the situation?

_____

_____

_____

_____

_____

_____

What would make you happy?

_____

_____

_____

_____

_____

_____

What negative consequences might take place if you did what made you happy?

_____

_____

_____

_____

_____

_____

_____

What might prevent you from doing what would make you happy?

_____

_____

_____

_____

_____

_____

What has to happen before you can do what would make you happy?

_____

_____

_____

_____

_____

_____

How would your life be different if you did what would make you happy?

_____

_____

_____

_____

_____

_____

_____

_____

_____

_____

_____

_____

_____

_____

4 DON'T MAKE IT PERSONAL

One day a farmer's donkey fell down an old dry well. For hours the animal cried wretchedly as the farmer tried to figure out what to do. Finally the farmer decided that the animal was old and not worth the trouble of rescuing, and that the well needed to be covered anyway. He invited all his neighbors to come over, grab a shovel, and help him fill the well with dirt.

At first as the well began to fill up, the donkey cried even more loudly. Then, to everyone's surprise, he quieted down.

The shoveling continued, and after some time the farmer looked down into the well. He was astonished at what he saw—as each shovelful of dirt hit the donkey's back, the donkey was shaking it off, tamping it down, and letting the dirt pile's growing height raise him toward the top of the well.

As soon as the pile of dirt brought the donkey to the top, he stepped over the well's stone rim and trotted away.

IF YOU NEED to remember how to cope when someone dumps on you, think of that patient, resourceful old donkey.

This chapter is all about how we take things personally and then deal with the consequences of that perspective—getting defensive, or launching into pitched battles over right and wrong. But it's also about growing a thicker skin and learning the communication skills and strategies that can move you beyond defensiveness and into a stance of self-control, self-confidence, and self-respect.

Taking Things Personally

When you take someone's anger-provoking behavior personally, you feel offended and disrespected. Your reaction to your uncomfortable feelings is either to defend yourself or to submit passively to what the other person seems to think of you. Either way, you view the other person's behavior as a literal, serious, personal threat to your well-being:

- In traffic, your blood pressure shoots up as you fume about the sloppiness of other drivers and about how their recklessness is putting you personally at risk.
- At the office, you take a colleague's disagreement with you as personal disrespect or hostility.
- Closer to home, your girlfriend goes off the deep end over some silly joke you told at a party, and you feel personally attacked and hurt.

In reality, however, reckless drivers drive recklessly whether you're on the road or not. Your colleagues at the office can disagree with you for reasons of their own that have nothing to do with you. And maybe your girlfriend is upset because the way you told that joke brought back some painful memory that you know nothing about. In each case, what you're taking personally isn't personal at all.

It's Not Always About You

How has taking things personally contributed to your anger?

_____

_____

_____

_____

_____

_____

_____

_____

_____

_____

_____

_____

_____

_____

_____

_____

_____

_____

_____

_____

Let me give you another kind of example. A client of mine was deeply in love with a woman who wasn't emotionally available. She would draw him in and then do something to push him away. (This is what's commonly called *sabotaging the relationship*.) At first he took her behavior personally because he had behaved badly toward her a few times and felt guilty. But as he and I talked and as he looked at his past behavior, he expressed deep sorrow. He worked on forgiving himself, and he apologized to the woman he loved. She accepted his apology, but soon enough she was pushing him away again. He was finally able to see that she had major issues around emotional intimacy, and that her pushing him away wasn't any type of personal statement about him. She'd had a pretty tough life, and the way she protected herself whenever she felt unsafe with someone was to go on the attack or withdraw. And her protective technique was highly effective!

You may never know the real reasons why people in your life have attacked you or withdrawn from you. They may have been suffering from the effects of past abuse, or other problems of their own may have played a role. What you can know is that their provocative behavior was almost certainly not personal, and so it would be a mistake for you to take it personally.

Making It Personal: A Clinical Example

Brian was an employee at a midsize corporation. Lately his boss, Lucas, had been directing more and more complaints and insults at Brian, and Brian was having a hard time not taking Lucas's behavior personally. As the situation grew worse, Brian was told to get counseling if he wanted to keep his job.

Therapist: Why do you take's Lucas's criticism personally?

Brian: How do you *not* take it personally when someone says you're a stupid, lazy liar who's not pulling his weight around the office?

Therapist: What does it mean when you take something personally?

Brian: It means I feel insulted and offended.

Therapist: What is that *feeling* called when you're insulted and offended?

Brian: I feel worthless.

Therapist: Are you telling me that Lucas's childish nonsense from the fourth grade is robbing you of your worth as a person?

Brian: Well, it *was* personal. He was looking right at me. How else should I react?

Therapist: That's the trick. They don't teach you how to cope with this stuff in school, do they?

Brian: I've learned to ignore it.

Therapist: It's one thing to ignore a dumb remark. It's quite another to ignore the loss of your worth as a person.

Brian: But it's not fair. I do a good job.

Therapist: Does arguing with Lucas's insults make things better?

Brian: No. I lost my cool, got written up, and now my job is sending me here or I'll be fired.

Therapist: Then Lucas was successful in dragging you down to his childish level with his schoolyard tactics. Your mistake is to take his kid stuff personally, which you can stop doing anytime you choose. You can also choose to see his insults as absurd nonsense and not take them seriously. If Lucas says the world is flat and the grass is pink, does that make it so? In a way, he's demonstrating that his arguments are bankrupt, and he's regressing to this absurd, childish level of debate because he's out of ammo. Once he pushed your buttons, he got some leverage. You were in pain and tore him down. Now he has confirmation of how unprofessional you can be. But now you know what he's up to. So the next time Lucas antagonizes you, you can shift gears. You can detach and disengage emotionally from his provocations. You can choose not to take his false accusations seriously, as if they made sense, and as if they were an accurate evaluation of your worth as a person.

Brian: I can always walk away.

Therapist: Yes. That's called disengaging with your feet.

Brian: What if he says, "Brian, you're such a dumbass."

Therapist: You're not required to prove to him how smart you are. How did he get to be the final judge over you? He's also human, and he has his own standards and preferences for how things ought to be. You don't have to be perfectly smart. You're smart enough as you are. You're worthwhile in spite of your mistakes.

Brian: What if he says something that's true—like that I really did forget to check the inventory before ordering a part?

Therapist: It only proves that you are an imperfect human being. It's a mistake, not a failure. You can say, "I get upset, too, when I make mistakes." It's not a crime to make a mistake, so it's not a matter of assigning guilt, fault, and blame. It's a matter of human imperfection. The issue isn't that you made a mistake. The issue is how you can fix it.

Brian: What if he says something bad about the company?

Therapist: Lucas knows all your soft spots, doesn't he? He knows that you're a loyal employee and that he can provoke you by bad-mouthing the company. You don't have to take that personally, either. You can remind yourself that his words are just smoke and mirrors for his own pain. Remind yourself that he has his own opinions and preferences, based on his own unique experiences and expectations. They're not right or wrong. They're just a matter of his own personal taste. You can remind yourself that you get to define yourself, using your own judgment, and that you can validate your efforts even if the outcomes aren't perfect. And if you want to disarm Lucas by doing something unexpected, you can agree with him when he points out that you made a mistake. You can say, "It's just awful, isn't it?"

Brian: Shouldn't I try to prevent it from happening again?

Therapist: There's no way to prevent imperfect human beings from being imperfect.

Brian: I've done a lot of favors for Lucas. He doesn't appreciate all the breaks I've given him.

Therapist: It's not fair. Do you take that personally, too?

Brian: Sure I do.

Therapist: So you're angry with him for his lack of consideration. It's unfair when he doesn't reciprocate your consideration on his behalf. Who else are you angry with?

Brian: Myself, for being such a chump. How can I stop feeling this way?

Therapist: By no longer defining your self-worth in terms of winning other people's approval or being appreciated for what you do. Whether Lucas appreciates you or not, you are a worthwhile human being, in spite of your faults and imperfections. You don't have to prove anything. You don't need a gold star for meeting someone else's expectations. It's nice to gain others' approval, but it's not a requirement. Lucas doesn't get to make the final evaluation of you as a human being. Your performance at work varies from hour to hour and from day to day, and you make the best decisions you can with the information available to the time. But you don't behave helpfully toward others just to get their approval. You do it because you value generosity and because your judgment tells you that it's good to help out. It's regrettable that you're not being appreciated, but you get to be the judge of how good is good enough. You didn't do anything wrong.

Brian: No. I didn't.

Therapist: You are not dependent on Lucas for the validation of your worth as a person. You have the power, right now, to validate your own efforts, your own judgment, and your own worth as a human being.

Brian: It still makes me angry.

Therapist: Then you can choose to tell him the truth, like a grown-up. You can say, "It makes me angry when you say that."

Brian: What if he says he doesn't care?

Therapist: That makes you even angrier. You can say, "You just made it worse. I'm angrier now than I was before."

Brian: What if he says he's angry with me?

Therapist: You can validate his anger, which is a legitimate human emotion. You can say, "I don't blame you for being angry. I get angry, too, when things don't go my way. I'm sorry you're angry, but I'm still angry, too."

Brian: Why should I say I'm sorry? I didn't do anything.

> **Others' antagonism is no reflection of your worth as a person, and you require no defense.**

Therapist: You're not expressing guilt. Guilt implies that you're taking ownership of a problem. You're expressing regret that Lucas is angry. Regret is the wish that things could be other than how they are. You can regret that Lucas is angry and in pain without taking ownership of his anger. Lucas's anger is his problem, not yours.

Brian: But what if he says that it's my fault and I was wrong?

Therapist: You hate to be in the wrong, don't you? But, once again, it's not a matter of right and wrong. The idea that right and wrong are absolutes is a carryover from childhood. Now, as an adult, you can live between those two extremes. Your human imperfections make people angry sometimes, and they may mismanage their anger. It's regrettable when they do that, and you can express regret about it. You can acknowledge Lucas's anger without condoning it, and you'll be setting an example for him to see and follow, if he chooses.

Brian: Lucas really does know how to push my buttons, doesn't he?

Therapist: He uses your vulnerabilities against you. But the more you give yourself credit for your own efforts, the less you'll rely on others for validation. By acknowledging your successes yourself, you'll come to respect yourself as a worthwhile human being. In time, you'll develop a thicker skin and be less vulnerable to Lucas's provocations.

BE LIKE A PACHYDERM

The Greek word *pachydermos* comes from *pachys* (thick) and *derma* (skin), so a pachyderm is a thick-skinned creature. The elephant, rhinoceros, and hippopotamus are all pachyderms, and their thick skins serve them well. Insects go after them, but once they discover they can't land a bite or get what they want, they move on to another target.

What about you? How well do you resist other people's biting words? When others behave in hurtful ways, do you take their behavior as an indication of your worth? Here are some ways to take things less personally and grow a thicker skin.

- **See another person's antagonism for what it is—a childish act intended to gain attention or relieve pain.** It has nothing to do with you, so it doesn't deserve attention or energy. Are you going to let your anger control your response to another person's immaturity? Or will you use your judgment to manage your hurt and anger in an appropriate way?

- **Don't defend yourself against insults or other hurtful behavior.** Your attackers aren't interested in your point of view. They're focused on relieving their own emotional pain, at your expense. Others' antagonism is no reflection of your worth as a person, and you require no defense.

- **Don't worry about looking or sounding stupid.** If someone asks you a question and you don't know the answer, you can say, "I need to think about that and get back to you." Remind yourself that you're an imperfect human being, you're allowed to make mistakes, and you do many things quite well. You will never be superior or inferior, but equal.

- **Put less focus on yourself.** Instead, think about your goals and the steps needed to meet them. In a social interaction, think about how to make the experience itself enjoyable, and ask yourself what you can do to feel more comfortable.

- **When someone attacks you, muster up the courage to risk doing something new.** For example, you can simply say, "I don't know what you're trying to accomplish." That's not a counterattack. It's just the truth. And if you feel good afterward, savor that feeling—you will have earned it.

Brian: Why does he behave that way?

Therapist: Because he doesn't respect himself. He's trying to relieve the pain of his own self-doubt by building himself up at your expense.

Brian: That doesn't work.

Therapist: That's why he has to keep doing it! If it worked, he could stop.

Brian: How can I get him to stop?

Therapist: Do you see how you're defining the problem in terms of changing Lucas? It's not about how you can get him to respond differently. How Lucas behaves is up to Lucas. It's more important to focus on what you can control. You can choose to stop trying to make things happen, or keep them from happening. You can decide instead to live in the present by focusing on what's real, not on what's potential. Instead of changing Lucas—which he hasn't asked you to do, and which wouldn't work anyway—you can change yourself. That's your right and your responsibility. When you change yourself, other people often pick up on that and treat you differently, like an equal member of the human race. As far as Lucas is concerned, you can disengage from his antagonism and emotionally detach yourself from his nonsense. Your reactions are only reinforcing his antagonism. When he sees that his provocations are running off you like water off a duck's back, he'll leave you alone.

Brian: But what will he do then?

Therapist: He might go and find himself another pushover. Or he might start following your example of self-respect, whether or not he knows that's what he's doing. He might even begin cooperating with you.

As we saw in the clinical example from chapter 3, Gabriel needed to learn that cooperating with his wife didn't mean submitting to her every whim. Here, Brian faced constant antagonism from his boss, even though his behavior at work was already cooperative. Despite the contrast in their situations, both men were coming to understand the same truth—that we all have the power to define ourselves and set our own standards for success, instead of vainly attempting to live up to someone else's standard. (We'll have more to say about standards in chapter 5.)

Getting Defensive

Have you ever been involved in an argument like this one between Antoine and Maria?

Maria: Antoine, you're late.

Antoine: I'm not late. You told me to come at 8:00.

Maria: No, I didn't. You're always making things up!

Antoine: No, I'm not. And I'm right on time.

Maria: Antoine, why can't you admit you're wrong?

Antoine: I didn't do anything! *You're* the liar.

Maria: Why are you getting so defensive?

Antoine: I'm not getting defensive!

Maria: You are! You're defending yourself right now.

Antoine: No, I'm not.

Here's what's going on for Antoine:

- He takes Maria's comment that he's late as a personal attack.
- He understands their argument to be not just about what time he was supposed to arrive, but also about his innocence of Maria's accusation, and therefore about his personal integrity and worth.
- He believes that if he doesn't argue in defense of his integrity and worth, he'll be accepting not only responsibility for Maria's unhappiness, but guilt, fault, and blame for being late as well.

Maybe Antoine was late, and maybe he wasn't. It doesn't matter. The real issue here is his anger with Maria over being falsely accused of being late. As long as Antoine takes Maria's accusation as a personal attack, he won't be able to respond with anything but defensiveness, and their conflict will continue to escalate.

Often when you become defensive in an argument, it's because you think you need to "do the right thing" by straightening the other person out and correcting his or her misperceptions of you. But what you don't see is that straightening the other person out is not your job—and your defensive arguments can't get that job done anyway. What your defensive lashing out does instead is build a protective wall around your heart so you can seal off your emotional pain.

WHO'S RIGHT? WHO'S WRONG?

As we've just seen, when you take things personally you can end up pleading your case to defend yourself against someone's false accusations. But your mistake is to take these accusations literally, personally, and seriously. When you do, you effectively choose to go before an imaginary court of law with a judge and jury of one. Once you're in that court, you're compelled to offer evidence of your innocence: "What do you mean, I never listen? You said to call the plumber, and I did. Here— look at the phone bill!" You may even call an expert witness to the stand: "I *don't* always blame you! Ask my brother—he'll tell you." But these courtroom maneuvers rarely cause the other person to have a change of mind, so your pleas are all in vain. You fail to make your case, and that failure only compounds your pain and escalates the miscommunication as you retaliate with angry accusations of your own.

Or consider the word *should,* as when someone says, "You should have done it this way." That word implies that the other person knows best—and the other person may indeed know best. But when you take the word *should* as an accusation that you're guilty of being wrong and need to be punished, you end up right back in that imaginary courtroom with all your reasons, facts, and defenses. When you take the word *should* as an indication of your personal incompetence and inadequacy, you play your part in turning a disagreement between equals into a fight about dominance and submission as you lose track of every question except *Who's right?* and *Who's wrong?*

Instead, try hearing the word *should* as simply expressing the other person's preference for a particular method of doing something. He or she is entitled to have preferences, just as you are. You're not guilty if you don't share someone else's preferences, and you don't need to defend yourself. And if it turns out that the other person's preference for a particular method really does reflect greater experience and skill, then you can make a clear decision about whether that person's preference is one you will also adopt, since the two of you will be talking about personal experience and opinions, not objective matters of right and wrong.

COMMON MISTAKES IN COMMUNICATION

Healthy communication about a difficult subject doesn't have to end in agreement. In fact, one benefit of regular conversation with someone who doesn't agree with you is the discovery that your disagreement can actually be stimulating to both of you.

But open-mindedness is essential. Each of you must be willing to listen to what the other is saying. When you find yourself in a conversation with someone else about a sensitive and potentially explosive subject, do you make any of the following common mistakes?

- **Talking too much.** When you need to talk with someone about a difficult personal problem between the two of you, it's possible that you'll begin by talking around the subject—being vague, trying to be polite, and hoping that your listener will somehow pick up your meaning. There's also the risk that as you talk and talk, you'll say something that the listener will react to defensively. But the fewer words you use to open the conversation and explain the problem as you see it, the better off you both will be.

- **Assuming that you have all the facts.** When you feel strongly about something, you're usually convinced that you have all the facts and know exactly what's what. You're also quite sure that you know who's right (you) and who's wrong (the other person), so you go into the conversation primarily to get the other person to agree with you. Then, the more the other person resists (perhaps in an effort to offer his or her own viewpoint), the harder you push to get your way. But you rarely, if ever, know all the facts, and you can't always be right. Go into the conversation prepared to listen to and consider the other person's point of view. And show that you're listening by nodding, saying "I see," and rephrasing the other person's key points ("So what you're saying is . . ."). The purpose of repeating what the other person has said in your own words is not to be a parrot but to create communication and dialogue, not to mention to give yourself a way to remember what the two of you talked about.

- **Not seeing your own role in the problem.** It's tempting to see every problem as someone else's fault. But if you're involved in the situation, then you're part of the problem in some way, and you need to remember that your role is at least as great as the other person's.

- **Jumping right into action.** When a problem is difficult, it's tempting to offer an immediate solution so the conversation can end quickly. But slow down. You need to hear the other person's side of the story, and the other person needs to know that his or her opinions and feelings have been heard. If you push too quickly for your own solution, the other person probably won't be committed to it, and the outcome will show that disengagement. You'll think you've solved the problem, only to find that nothing has changed and you're quickly back to square one.

- **Not understanding the importance of how you sound.** The feeling conveyed in your voice will have more of an impact and be remembered longer than the words you actually speak. If you yell, you may think you're forcing the other person to listen, but what's more likely is that he or she is waiting for you to pause so they can lash out with a defense against your verbal attack. Raising your voice creates the kind of stress and tension that provoke anger. The louder your voice, the more intense the anger, and the greater the risk of a physical confrontation. Be sure to modulate your voice so that its volume and tone don't deliver a message of aggression or dominance.

- **Being oblivious to personal space.** You can make the other person uneasy if you stand or sit too close. But if you stand or sit too far away, you can come off as cold and uncaring. Watch the other person's movement toward you, and especially away from you, for clues to getting the distance right. If you see that you're too close, pull back a little.

- **Not understanding your purpose in communicating.** Ask yourself what you hope to achieve by talking with someone else about a difficult problem between the two of you. Do you see the conversation as your chance to win an argument? Or is it about finding a solution and deeper understanding? If all you want to do is prove something, get even, or make yourself look good, then that's not communication—it's grandstanding.

Defensiveness and Good Intentions

How has defensiveness contributed to your anger?

_____

_____

_____

_____

_____

_____

_____

_____

When have you thought it was your job to argue against someone else's mistaken perception of you?

_____

_____

_____

_____

_____

_____

_____

_____

Getting Beyond Defensiveness

You can take concrete steps to reduce your defensiveness in the face of others' criticism or attacks. For one thing, you can learn to talk about your feelings instead of arguing the "facts" of your "case." You can also choose not to antagonize the other person. You can actively take control of the real-life choices that you have in the present, and you can learn to detach yourself emotionally from an anger-provoking situation. In addition, when you say or do something unexpected in response to someone else's criticism or hurtful behavior, or when you respond in a way that validates the other person's emotional reality, you can disarm a critic or attacker while protecting yourself nondefensively.

DON'T ARGUE YOUR CASE

Let me tell you about Mr. and Mrs. R, a couple I recently saw in my office. When they came in, they recounted an argument they'd had the previous Friday. They'd started the day in bed, cuddling and snuggling affectionately. But then Mr. R felt his wife resisting. He snapped at her, and she got defensive. Mr. R let out a big sigh and got out of bed. They ate breakfast in silence. When Mr. R got home from work that evening, Mrs. R was in the kitchen.

Mr. R: What's for dinner?

Mrs. R: Meat loaf.

Mr. R: Meat loaf? Again? We have meat loaf every Friday.

Mrs. R: You like meat loaf. You've never asked for anything different on Friday.

Mr. R: It would be nice, just once, to have something different—like a salmon steak.

Mrs. R: I don't like salmon. You know that.

Mr. R: But *I* like salmon. And you might like salmon more than you think you do, if you'd ever give it a try.

As Mr. and Mrs. R related this exchange, they told me that it had been marked by particular intensity. They didn't understand why they'd been so upset, and neither one knew why the other had made such a fuss about something as trivial as meat loaf or salmon. I explained that their explicit disagreement had been about meat loaf and the routine of dinner, but their true argument was about their feelings, and it had to do with that morning's unresolved emotional tension. It's important to understand that ignoring or hiding feelings creates tension in relationships.

FOCUS ON FEELINGS, NOT FACTS

Talking about your emotions simply and clearly can leave you feeling vulnerable, but it's one of the most important skills you can develop as you learn to manage your anger. Here are some ineffective strategies that you may be using when a disagreement arises between you and someone else:

- **Protesting your innocence.** "But I didn't do it—I swear to God!"
- **Giving orders.** "Get ahold of yourself. Back off. Leave me alone."
- **Taking too much responsibility for others.** "Let me do it. You're just screwing it up."
- **Predicting the future.** "If you don't stop now, there's going to be trouble."
- **Appealing to logic.** "Be reasonable. Use your head!"
- **Trying to force agreement.** "You're wrong. That's totally false."
- **Denying the legitimacy of the other person's feelings.** "You have no right to be angry at me after all I've done for you."
- **Resorting to sarcasm or ridicule.** "Wow, you sure look beautiful with your face all red like that."

How has protesting your innocence contributed to your anger?

_____

_____

_____

_____

_____

How has giving orders contributed to your anger?

_____

_____

_____

_____

_____

_____

How has taking too much responsibility for others contributed to your anger?

_____

_____

_____

_____

_____

_____

How has predicting the future contributed to your anger?

_____

_____

_____

_____

_____

_____

How has appealing to logic contributed to your anger?

_____

_____

_____

_____

_____

_____

_____

How has trying to force agreement contributed to your anger?

_____

_____

_____

_____

_____

_____

_____

How has denying the legitimacy of other people's feelings contributed to your anger?

_____

_____

_____

_____

_____

_____

_____

How has resorting to sarcasm or ridicule contributed to your anger?

_____

_____

_____

_____

_____

_____

AVOID ANTAGONISM

We've talked about antagonism as critical, blaming, or intimidating behavior designed to get attention and relieve the antagonist's emotional pain. When you're angry, your logical thought processes are swept away by a wave of emotion and defensiveness. You're vulnerable to others' antagonistic behavior, and you're likely to return it—with interest. But you'll sabotage your happiness if you engage in this tug-of-war. If your antagonist can't behave like an adult, then being the adult in the room will be up to you.

But before you can respond effectively to someone else's anger, you have to be able to identify and relieve your own. You have to give yourself emotional first aid. You have to stop your own bleeding before you can even begin to think straight. Men aren't always used to putting themselves first in their own lives, but it's entirely appropriate to make yourself your first priority in conditions of combat. That's not being selfish—being selfish means taking care of number one and letting everyone else be damned. Giving yourself emotional first aid means taking care of yourself so you can be there for others as a good husband, father, son, brother, friend, or employee.

If you can manage your anger, you can behave like a self-respecting adult no matter how poorly other people manage their own anger. But if you can't manage your anger, you'll be setting yourself up to be antagonized again and again.

Being the Adult in the Room

How has others' antagonism contributed to your anger?

_____

_____

_____

_____

_____

_____

_____

_____

_____

Was there ever a time when you avoided getting pulled into a tug-of-war with an antagonist? How did you do that?

_____

_____

_____

_____

_____

_____

_____

_____

_____

TAKE CONTROL OF YOUR CHOICES

The antidote to feeling defensive is to understand that you're in control of your choices in the present. To take positive control over these choices, you have to make an active effort. For example, the next time you're angry, remind yourself that you have choices now that you didn't have as a child. As a child, you sought to get control in the wrong way—by losing your temper or suppressing your anger. But now, as an adult, you can choose to express your anger by simply and clearly saying how you're feeling rather than arguing, shouting, or defending yourself. You can respond from a place of self-respect instead of reacting from a place of rage and defensiveness.

When someone hurts you, you always have options about how to respond. You may think you don't, but the reality is that you simply don't like your options.

LEARN DETACHMENT

When you separate other people from their behavior, you're practicing detachment. Learning to detach yourself emotionally from a situation often starts with learning to take a moment before reacting to someone else's provocations. In that moment, you can ask yourself whether the provocative behavior is directed at you personally, or whether it might be coming from the other person's fear, anger, or pain. If you can make this kind of distinction, you can create more emotional distance between yourself and others' behavior. But it's important to remember that practicing detachment is not the same as building a wall. Your goal is to heal yourself and your relationships with other human beings, not to coldly distance yourself from others, and especially not to set up barriers between yourself and the people who matter most to you.

When you're provoked to anger by someone's words or behavior, step back the same way you would if the person were coughing or sneezing.

Choices and Control

How has the sense of being out of control contributed to your anger?

_____

_____

_____

_____

_____

_____

_____

_____

_____

_____

_____

_____

_____

_____

_____

_____

_____

_____

DO THE UNEXPECTED

Always remind yourself that antagonists are seeking attention and trying in their own dysfunctional way to heal their own pain. That reminder in turn can help you remember not to take their hurtful behavior personally, and not to take their words at face value. Since an antagonist isn't really interested in what you're feeling or thinking, you always have the option of keeping your feelings and thoughts to yourself. But choosing not to defend yourself or return someone's antagonism doesn't mean passively allowing yourself to be a doormat. Instead, you can respond by making a statement that's true but neutral:

- **"It certainly seems like I'm hard to get along with."** You are not agreeing with the so-called facts of the matter. You're acknowledging the reality of how the other person apparently feels.
- **"It must make you angry when that happens. I don't blame you. In that situation, I'd be angry, too."** This is an appropriate validation of the other person's anger and of his or her worth as a person—and your own human worth. It also gives the other person a word, *angry*, for what he or she is feeling. And that can be very helpful because so many people have been taught that it's all right to be "upset," but never all right to be angry.
- **"I'm sorry you're so angry."** This is not an admission that you deserved the other person's angry outburst. It's an expression of appropriate regret that the other person is in so much emotional pain.
- **"It makes me angry when you blow up in my face for telling you how I feel."** That's just the truth about your response to the other person's behavior. You're not saying the other person is wrong—or right. And you're not defending yourself. You're just reporting what's going on for you.

These statements are not defenses. They're not counterattacks. They put you in control because you're the one choosing to create an atmosphere in which cooperation is possible, and that's the first step toward solving whatever the real problem turns out to be.

Here are a few more neutral statements that you can use to disarm a critic or attacker, avoid arguing about others' preferences or standards, and keep your own defensiveness at bay:

- "You have a real problem here. I don't know what to tell you."
- "It's just awful, isn't it?"
- "I don't know how you stand it."
- "I never thought of it that way."
- "You may have a point."
- "That would be nice, wouldn't it?"
- "It seems that way sometimes, doesn't it?"
- "I know you mean well and want what's best for me, but I prefer to do it this way."
- "Thanks for calling that to my attention."
- "I'm sure you'll think of something."
- "I can tell you're angry—you're shouting."
- "That's one theory, isn't it?"
- "I hear what you're saying. I appreciate it, and I'll be fine."
- "I totally agree—I'm just not sure it would help."

Statements like these don't really even have to make sense. You're using them to set limits, both on other people's behavior and on your own defensiveness. But here's the key: *Never make such a statement in a provocative or antagonistic way.* Speak slowly, softly, deliberately, and clearly, and keep your tone neutral.

5 TAKE RESPONSIBILITY FOR YOUR ANGER

TO LIVE A healthy and happy life, you have to deal with your anger. This chapter explores the negative consequences of focusing too much on others and depending on their approval to feel good about yourself. The chapter also looks at the growth and power that come from focusing on yourself and your own happiness, knowing and asking for what you want, and setting your own standards for self-worth.

Taking Responsibility for Others

Most men are responsible for themselves. They pay their bills, show up at work, and brush their teeth.

But some men take it a step further and also assume responsibility for others' happiness and welfare. Whether that means solving someone else's problems, cheering someone up, calming someone down, mediating a dispute, making others see the error of their ways, curing the sick, or raising the dead, these men are convinced that the buck stops with them.

But others aren't always interested in having their problems solved, or being cheered up or calmed down, or otherwise opening their lives to these excessively responsible men's interventions. Then these men tell themselves that no one appreciates their hard work and sacrifices, and that makes them angry. They feel like failures for not pleasing the people they want to help, and that makes them angry, too.

It's an understandable reaction for men who are shouldering a "have to" burden. They "have to" help others overcome adversity. In fact, they actually have to *prevent* adversity so that nothing bad ever happens to them or anyone else. Naturally, they have to make sure that everyone around them is fully informed of every possible contingency, since misfortune can't be prevented if everyone isn't pulling in the same direction—the direction that just happens to be the one these men think is best. So who could possibly blame them for feeling resentful about the unfairness of it all? After everything they've tried to do for others, they finally decide they've had enough of other people's irresponsibility and ingratitude.

Some of these men fall into the cycle of excessive responsibility leading to resentment and anger because they're not just shouldering a "have to" burden, but also carrying a load of guilt from the past, and they want to avoid the pain of taking on any more. They're also compelled to prove their innocence in any and all circumstances and escape punishment by offering elaborate, lengthy accountings and justifications of their behavior and intentions. Other members of this excessively responsible group of men are trying not to displease people they depend on for approval and validation as a human being. In both cases, what these men believe to be a selfless, positive focus on others' welfare turns out to be a self-focused, negative enterprise aimed at keeping their own imperfections under wraps and avoiding punishment for what is invariably a misconceived sense of guilt.

Do you know any men like these? Is it possible that you are one?

- When you're confronted with evidence that you are not perfect, do you become snappish, hypercritical, argumentative, defensive, or withdrawn? Do you resort to giving others the silent treatment?
- Do you believe that perfect people never lose control?
- Do you believe that perfect people know everything, that they can accurately predict the future, and that they never allow bad things to happen?
- Do you believe that perfect people never fail to please others because they can read others' minds?
- Do you believe that perfect people never get angry?

Had Enough of "Have To"?

What's in your "have to" burden?

_____
_____
_____
_____
_____
_____
_____
_____
_____

When have you tried to prevent bad things from happening?

_____
_____
_____
_____
_____
_____
_____
_____
_____

When have you felt guilty or misunderstood?

_____

_____

_____

_____

_____

_____

_____

_____

_____

When have you made sacrifices and sought others' approval?

_____

_____

_____

_____

_____

_____

_____

_____

_____

If so, you'll be riding on the merry-go-round of excessive responsibility, resentment, and anger until you choose to explore your thinking, drop your "have to" burden and imaginary guilt, and take on the weight of true responsibility for yourself and for your own standards. You can try living others' lives and solving others' problems. You can even come up with life plans and solutions that should suit others to a T. In reality, though, your plans and solutions won't work for others, because you don't actually know what's best for them. You don't know how to live others' lives or solve their problems—you have your hands full with your own.

> **You don't know how to live others' lives or solve their problems—you have your hands full with your own.**

It's Not Fair!

How many men are silently tormented by their sense that life and the world are unfair? It's a thought that arises when they're forced to put up with rude behavior in a public setting, or listen to a family member's sarcastic response to a sincere offer of help, or watch as an undeserving coworker is promoted to the executive suite.

The sense of what is and isn't fair is one of the most common legacies from childhood, that time when you first learned about sharing and taking your turn and playing by the rules. Now, in adulthood, it's perfectly obvious to you that some people have far more advantages and far greater privilege than others, and that the rules don't apply equally to everyone.

Focusing on what's fair and what isn't means focusing on the way things should be rather than on the way things actually are. We can all agree that things should be fair, but we won't always agree on just what fairness means in a particular situation. If you're struggling with anger, you may tend to believe that fairness means getting your way in a conflict, and when you don't get your way, you may become angry over what you see as the unfairness of the outcome. You may also see it as your responsibility to make other people understand that the outcome is unfair because it doesn't meet your standard of fairness, and you may decide that you have to straighten others out by enforcing your standard. When others ignore your standard and don't respond in the way you want, you may feel cheated—the core experience of unfairness. So you unleash your anger and try forcing others to change. You may even feel the urge to use weapons—the verbal weapons of yelling and threats, or the physical weapons of your fists or a gun. The circumstances that inflamed your sense of unfairness were probably not of earthshaking importance, but unfairness feels like such a primal violation that it can lead to relatively grave consequences.

If you believe that someone who treats you unfairly is challenging your worth as a human being, then you can question that belief. It shows that you need other people's approval and acceptance before you can feel good about yourself. But other people don't possess superior knowledge about you or your worth, and they really don't know what's best for you. Their opinions reflect their own personal preferences, not some objective measure of your human worth. Instead of dwelling on how to please other people, you can choose to deal with the underlying problem—the notion that you need to become a better person in their eyes, a person even more responsible for their happiness and welfare than your own, before you can be deemed worthy.

What does the concept of fairness mean to you?

_____

_____

_____

_____

When have you felt angry about something that was unfair?

_____

_____

_____

_____

_____

Choosing Your Own Happiness

If you don't choose your own happiness, who will? Unfortunately, lots of men are not used to doing just that. They don't trust their own judgment, and so they feel obligated to depend on the supposedly superior judgment of others. But making deliberate choices on your own behalf is an act of control.

Why not go ahead and do something that you would normally pass up out of concern about what others might think? You can decide that you have as much right to do it as anyone else does. You can catch yourself as you're about to discount it as scary, pointless, or frivolous. You can also catch yourself as you're about to reject an opportunity to do something just because you might not do it perfectly. You can tell yourself that you don't have to be perfect.

Don't let obstacles, problems, criticism, expectations, or failures in your past keep you from making the choice to change for the better.

IMPROVE YOURSELF, NOT OTHERS

An excessively responsible man may act as if he thinks he's fine just the way he is, and he may protect his self-created veneer of perfection by denying any evidence to the contrary—he doesn't make mistakes, he knows everything, he isn't weak, he's never wrong. He's also exempt from guilt, fault, and blame. This man wants what he wants when he wants it, and he doesn't hesitate to demand that others submit to his wishes, especially when it's "for their own good." And when he doesn't get what he wants, it's because others are falling down on the job. It's up to him to set them straight, and he'll use every manipulative trick in the book to do it:

- Guilt trips ("After all I've done for you . . .") when he feels that others don't appreciate the amount of responsibility he takes for their happiness
- Appeals to "the principle of the thing," even though he can't actually say what the principle is
- Appeals to fairness, defined as getting what he wants
- Threats and intimidation ("You'll be sorry . . .") to ensure that he gets what he wants now, and the next time as well.

But these attitudes are powerful defenses against the painful truth that all people, himself included, are both unique and imperfect. His defenses allow him to maintain a facade of superiority. And yet a man who takes too much responsibility for others actually feels inferior, inadequate, worthless, and guilty. That makes him angry, so he relieves his anger by trying to turn the inferior, inadequate, ungrateful people in his life into people who won't disappoint him anymore.

Meanwhile, a different man may attempt to relieve his painful feelings of inadequacy and inferiority by revving up his quest to meet others' standards. But it's a struggle. When he tries to motivate himself to change by comparing himself to more successful friends and relatives, the comparisons only confirm his negative self-talk. And when he tries to motivate himself with self-criticism for the mistakes he's made in attempting to please others, he once again confirms the painful feelings of inferiority, inadequacy, and worthlessness.

If you believe that others can't get along without your help and your standards, then you'll see others as unworthy of respect until they've achieved some unobtainable degree of perfection. And if you believe that you have a responsibility to uphold the standards of people you're trying to please, then you'll see yourself as unworthy of respect until you've achieved some unobtainable degree of perfection. Either way, you'll be concealing your self-doubts behind a facade of anger that is likely to find inappropriate expression.

> Most men never question the deep beliefs they formed as children. Those beliefs aren't even rational, and they're not accessible to the conscious mind. They lurk in a man's psyche, waiting for just the right time to kick in and drag him down.

HOW GOOD IS GOOD ENOUGH?

There's nothing wrong with trying to better yourself. We all want to be better than we are—smarter, happier, wittier, more popular, more lovable, more successful, richer, and even thinner. Why settle for being less than all you can be?

But here's the trap. When you say, "Life will better if . . ." or "I will be more successful when . . . ," you imply that you are less than your best self right now. And if you believe that you always have to be better than you are, it can be hard to find the motivation to improve since you may not be able to find the middle ground between being perfect and feeling worthless. After all, you can't run a successful race when the finish line keeps moving farther and farther away from you.

When have you tried to better yourself?

Did you do it because you wanted to or because someone else wanted you to?

What are your standards for yourself . . .

As a father?

_____

_____

_____

_____

_____

As a son?

_____

_____

_____

_____

_____

As a husband?

_____

_____

_____

_____

_____

As a brother?

_____

_____

_____

_____

_____

As an employee?

_____

_____

_____

_____

_____

Where did these standards come from?

_____

_____

_____

_____

_____

Improvement or Perfection?
A Clinical Example

Jack could not see why he shouldn't be hard on his wife and kids—it was for their own good, he thought. "I'm no harder on them than I am on myself," he would say. During his first session with his therapist, Jack explained that he often got angry with his family but always apologized afterward. His wife and children were not impressed by his apologies, however—they knew the whole scenario would play out again, and probably sooner than later.

The therapist listened to Jack talk about the circumstances that provoked his anger—the grocery bills racked up by his wife, his seven-year-old son's disrespectful behavior, his teenage daughter's irresponsibility—and asked a focusing question:

Therapist: What do all these anger-provoking situations have in common?

Jack: Nothing. They're all different.

Therapist: That's true. Your wife spends too much money on food, your son is rude, and your daughter is irresponsible. But is there a common denominator?

Jack: I don't see one.

Therapist: The common denominator of your anger at your wife and kids is that they make mistakes.

Jack: I don't have a problem with getting mad when they screw up.

Therapist: Well, you *should* have a problem with it because your anger at mistakes is making everyone miserable, even you.

Jack: Should I kiss my kids on the cheek for being disrespectful?

Therapist: Is there no middle ground between kissing and abusing? Do you see how scornful you are when people don't live up to your standard of perfection?

Jack: They can try, can't they?

Therapist: They've been trying all along. They just can't succeed. You've set them up for failure. Now they're angry, discouraged, and depressed.

Jack: What's wrong with wanting people to be right and not wrong?

Therapist: Quite a bit. You learned about right and wrong as a child. You wanted to avoid mistakes. But your understanding of mistakes was that of a child. And today your understanding is still immature and incomplete.

Jack: How can I change?

Therapist: That's a good question. We don't change by making New Year's resolutions. We change by taking appropriate actions in the real world.

Jack: What can I do when the kids do something wrong, or when my wife makes a mistake?

Therapist: It's not a matter of right or wrong. It's about accepting them and everyone else as imperfect. And if their imperfections make you angry, you can choose to say, "It makes me angry when you do that."

The following weekend, Jack took his wife and children sailing. As usual, nothing his family did was good enough, and that was especially true of his wife, who couldn't manage to tie a simple knot in the dock line after Jack eased the boat into the slip at the end of their day on the water.

"You're doing it wrong!" he yelled at her.

She untied the line and tried again.

"That's still no good!" Jack yelled again.

His wife, used to this behavior, sighed and gave it another try, and Jack was about to yell at her again when he stopped himself.

Wait a minute, he thought, *it's not wrong—it's just imperfect. Have I been doing this to her for our whole married life? My God—no one deserves to be treated like this.*

Jack apologized for yelling, and this time he really meant it.

KNOW WHAT PLEASES YOU—AND WHAT DOESN'T

The antidote to taking excessive responsibility for others and chafing at life's unfairness is to stop doing what makes you unhappy and start doing what brings you happiness. This often means allowing others to live with the consequences of their own choices. Someone in your life who has a problem can step up and ask you for help—or not. In the meantime, you can choose to stop trying to prevent future catastrophes and start taking life as it comes.

Just as others can choose to ask you for what they want, you're allowed to ask others for what you want. Asking someone for what you want isn't a sign of weakness or dependency. It's a matter of cooperation. It is a risk, however, because the other person can say no.

> **ASKING FOR WHAT YOU WANT** It's risky to ask other people for what you want since you never really know how they're going to respond. But adults can choose to take appropriate risks. That's what adults to do.

Trying to Change Others

When have you tried to change someone else?

_____

_____

_____

_____

_____

_____

What was the result?

_____

_____

_____

_____

_____

_____

What did you learn?

_____

_____

_____

_____

_____

_____

If you ask and get what you want, you'll have more confidence and a more optimistic outlook the next time you ask for something. And if the answer is no, avoid taking it personally. You can remember that your self-respect doesn't depend on getting what you want. Your human worth is not affected either way.

If someone's refusal or inability to grant your request makes you angry, you can express your legitimate anger in a truthful but civil way: "It makes me angry when I tell you what would make me happy and you won't give it to me." And if the other person's response is to cooperate with your wishes, that response deserves to be validated. This last point is important to keep in mind, since men dealing with anger often pay close attention to everything they don't like, but overlook or take for granted what's going well.

Before you can ask others to cooperate with you as you seek your own happiness, you have to know what makes you happy. Does worrying about what other people think make you happy? Fine! You can choose to continue. But if it makes you unhappy, you can choose to stop.

As you continue to make choices about what does and doesn't make you happy, it will probably occur to you that the simplest choice is to stop doing what makes you unhappy. For example, instead of continually nagging an employee about her inconsistent work performance, you can choose to say, "It makes me angry when you don't follow through. I would like you to show more consistency in your work." As for your own work, maybe it will make you happy to take a day off and do nothing. If so, you can choose to do that without resorting to self-accusations of irresponsibility or unproductivity. You can choose to see doing nothing as doing something—namely, taking a well-deserved, healing vacation from the strain of your many responsibilities.

> *Time for self-care is essential. If you don't take the time to do the things you want to do, you'll resent the important things you have to do.*

What Makes You Happy?

What is it that will make you happy?

_____

_____

_____

_____

_____

_____

What choices do you have for making your happiness a reality?

_____

_____

_____

_____

_____

What doesn't make you happy?

_____

_____

_____

_____

_____

Setting Personal Standards:
A Clinical Example

As we know, a lot of men can't make choices because they don't know what pleases them. They've often been so busy living up to others' standards that they haven't had the confidence to develop standards of their own. What follows is an account of how basing our self-esteem on others' standards affects our sense of happiness.

Lilly and Jason had been married for eight years. They were having some financial difficulties, and so they made an agreement to hold off on unnecessary purchases until they were out of debt.

One day Lilly was out shopping and spotted a watch that she loved. The price was $350, and she charged it to their credit card.

When Lilly showed Jason the watch, he exploded. "How could you? You know we're in debt!"

His outburst did nothing to solve the problem, of course. After all, he couldn't remove the charge from their credit card bill by yelling at his wife. So what was the point? What was Jason really angry about? Was it their financial situation? Lilly's purchase? The watch? All of the above?

In this case, the answer was none of the above.

Jason believed that a good husband was supposed to provide for his family without limits. Not being able to afford the watch Lilly wanted made him feel inferior. Therefore, he felt intensely guilty not only for lashing out at his wife but also for not being a better provider.

In his mind, the inability to afford everything his wife wanted made him a bad husband, no matter how hard he worked or how much he did around the house. And because he was a bad husband, Lilly would certainly leave him for someone who could afford to buy her nice things—a thought that sent Jason into a downward emotional spiral.

It wasn't fair! And if Jason really thought about it, the whole situation was Lilly's fault, and so were their financial problems. It wasn't his fault if he could never be enough! And it wouldn't be his fault when Lilly divorced him for not living up to her standards. He could already see her looking at him with contempt. And why not? He wasn't cutting it as a husband. How could he expect her to love him? But maybe there was something he could do to win her back. Maybe he could work even harder, do even more around the house, try in every way to meet her standards for a husband and provider . . .

At this point, Jason had a conversation with his therapist.

Jason: How can I get my wife to love me again? I've done everything I can think of.

Therapist: Do you see yourself as a good husband? You have to feel worthy of your wife's love before you can seek it from her.

Jason: Well, how do I feel worthy of my wife's love? I don't have a clue how to do that.

Therapist: You have to know what your own standards are for being a good husband.

Jason: I'm afraid of failing as a husband.

Therapist: What does it mean to be a successful husband?

Jason: I don't know . . . giving my wife everything she wants?

Therapist: Well, wants are endless. As soon as we get everything we want, we all want more.

Jason: Well . . . what, then?

Therapist: You have to have courage. Courage lets you take the risk of doing something hard—like setting your own standards for being a good husband, even though your wife might disapprove in some ways.

Jason: But I don't want to upset my wife. What if she leaves me?

Therapist: We don't know what the outcome will be. But if you have the courage to set your own standards for being a successful husband, you'll have a sense of accomplishment and maturity, and you'll have more self-confidence and greater self-respect, regardless of the outcome.

DEFINING SUCCESS

If you want to be successful, you have to know what success means to you. A six-figure income is a common measure of success for men, who learn early in life that their value in society, and as humans, is often judged by how much money they are able to make. But it's possible to define success in other ways. For example, you can take into consideration the amount of love and support you share with others, or the breadth of your talents and accomplishments, or the difference you make as a resident of your city or state.

If your world is small and safe, it will be a comfortable place for you to hang out, although you'll probably limit your options for growth since you won't be having many new experiences. By contrast, every time you take a step away from your comfort zone, you take a step toward your potential, which has no limits. But this effort entails dealing with fear on some level. This is where courage comes in.

HAVING COURAGE

Courage is the capacity and willingness to take something on even though it's hard or frightening. It requires you to trust your own judgment and risk being less than perfect, in order to solve actual problems rather than constantly trying to prevent disasters that may never even occur.

Making choices on your own behalf can be hard at first. But that struggle is the very thing that will lead to success. In fact, sometimes struggle is exactly what you need in your life. It teaches you the ability to take life as it comes and to do the best you can with it. That is true power and control—not too much and not too little, but just enough.

Success Is . . .

When have you felt successful?

_____

_____

_____

_____

_____

_____

_____

Choosing to Be Brave

When have you experienced courage?

_____

_____

_____

_____

_____

_____

_____

_____

_____

CONCLUSION

To end, I'll share two stories.

Two ducks were peacefully gliding along on a pond when suddenly one ventured too far into the other's territory. A fight started, fast, and it was furious. But after a few seconds, the ducks paddled off in separate directions, just as suddenly as they'd begun fighting. As they moved apart, they flapped their wings vigorously, and then they returned to gliding along as if the fight had never happened.

How did those two ducks return to such a peaceful state immediately after their fight? Why didn't they suffer afterward, the way most humans do? Why didn't they have any wounds to lick?

The answer is simple—when they flapped their wings, they worked off the energy and emotions that had built up during the fight. They felt their energy and emotions fully, and they purged the conflict fully. As a result, their fight didn't stick around to snarl their systems.

Why don't we humans, for all our supposed sophistication, adopt this simple wisdom from nature? We suffer all our lives, and we build up huge backlogs of energy and emotions. Unlike the two ducks, though, many of us don't purge our conflicts, and they become like physical wounds that never get a chance to heal. But fresh emotions are healthy when we feel them fully and express them properly.

We are all, in a sense, children of anger. When we were kids, every one of us saw our caregivers get angry. How they handled their anger when we were young had an impact on how we express our own feelings today. To a greater or lesser degree, our parents' anger taught us things about ourselves and about life, and many of those lessons were not positive. But those lessons shaped us anyway, undermining our good judgment and impairing our ability to see the world objectively. In fact, this childhood experience is so common that, as noted in a 2001 *Perspectives in Psychiatric Care* article on healthy anger management, people have fewer successful strategies for controlling anger than they do for controlling other strong emotional states, such as fear or sadness. And why wouldn't that be the case, when so few people, in their childhoods, had opportunities to see adults manage their anger in an intelligent way?

Intelligent anger management means transforming excessive physiological arousal, altering aggressive thoughts, and modifying unhealthy types of behavior that interfere with problem solving. It certainly doesn't mean eradication of anger, in my view. But even if complete elimination of anger were possible, it wouldn't be desirable—anger has self-protective functions such as maintaining boundaries and mobilizing the courage needed to correct injustices.

Have you ever heard that experience is the best teacher? My goal with this book has been to help you maximize the learning that you can gain from the experience of anger so you'll be better equipped to deal with future events. If experience is the best teacher, then the more you experience anger, the more you are able to learn. Therefore, even a raw outburst of strong anger may offer you ways to grow and develop. And that brings me to the second story.

There was once a man who set out to slay all the monsters in the world. Before long, he encountered the monster of suffering.

"No one wants to suffer," the man shouted, raising his sword. "You are worthless. Prepare to die!"

But the monster of suffering spoke softly to the man.

"I know that you think I cause needless pain and sorrow," the monster said. "You think the world would be better off without me. But one day when you were a boy, you put your hand too close to a flame. Do you remember?"

The man stood still for a moment, confused. But then a look of understanding crossed his face.

"Aha!" the man said.

He sheathed his sword, bowed to the monster, and returned to his home.

Aldous Huxley once said, "Experience is not what happens to a man. It is what a man does with what happens to him." Your experiences of the past affect what you do in the present—and, by the same token, you never know when an unexpected, frustrating event may lead to an equally unexpected but beautiful new experience. It's all in what you do with it.

APPENDIX:
CATCH YOURSELF IN THE ACT

Suffering is unavoidable, but even in an extremely difficult situation you can grow spiritually and take your difficulties as a test of your inner strength. You can look to future goals and rise above current sufferings as if they were already in the past. You can accept your challenges, be proud of your struggles, and suffer bravely.

Whether you obsess over past and possible misfortunes or use misfortune to grow stronger, the choice will be yours. Use it wisely. And as you practice managing your anger, use this table as a quick reference. Consult it when you need a reminder about how to handle yourself in an anger-provoking situation.

WHEN YOU CATCH YOURSELF . . .	REMIND YOURSELF . . .
Thinking *This is what I should do*.	The word *should* often indicates a preference, but it may not be your own preference.
Demanding others' submission for the sake of efficiency.	It's more productive to secure others' cooperation.
Trying to please others.	You don't know how they want to be pleased.
Trying not to displease others.	You can set and live up to your own standards.
Assuming more responsibility than the situation requires of you.	You can allow others to be responsible for themselves.
Protecting others from the consequences of their behavior.	They did not ask for your help.
Trying to prevent disaster.	You cannot predict the future or prevent things from happening, so it's better to take life as it comes.
Holding perfectionistic standards for yourself and others.	You don't really know what's best.
Trying to prove your worth to others.	Self-worth comes from within.
Blowing others' accusations out of proportion.	You can focus on the reality of the situation.
Reacting strongly to someone else's hurtful words.	You can validate the other person's feelings while choosing to see his or her hurtful words as merely absurd.
Becoming furious when something minor goes wrong.	It's an inconvenience or a disappointment, not the end of the world.
Defending yourself and protesting your innocence when someone is angry with you.	You are not the issue.

RESOURCES

The following organizations and other resources offer help and support for a variety of issues associated with anger management or with circumstances that can lead to problematic anger.

Professional Support

INDIVIDUAL THERAPEUTIC TREATMENT AND INFORMATION

American Psychiatric Association, Finder.psychiatry.org

Anxiety and Depression Association of America (ADAA), ADAA.org

Children and Adults with Attention-Deficit/Hyperactivity Disorder (CHADD), CHADD.org

Depression and Bipolar Support Alliance (DBSA), DBSAlliance.org

GoodTherapy.org

GriefShare, Griefshare.org

Mental Health America (MHA), Mentalhealthamerica.net

National Alliance on Mental Illness (NAMI), NAMI.org

National Eating Disorders Association (NEDA), Nationaleatingdisorders.org

PsychCentral, Psychcentral.com

Substance Abuse and Mental Health Services Association, SAMHSA.gov

TherapyTribe, Therapytribe.com

PREVENTION OF SELF-HARM AND SUICIDE

American Foundation for Suicide Prevention (AFSP), AFSP.org

Self-injury.net

Suicide Prevention Lifeline, 800-273-8255 (800-273-TALK), Suicidepreventionlifeline.org

HEALING FROM VIOLENCE/SEXUAL VIOLENCE

MenWeb, Batteredmen.com

National Child Abuse Hotline, 800-422-4453 (800-4-A-CHILD), Childhelp.org/hotline

National Domestic Violence Hotline, 800-799-7233 (800-799-SAFE), NDVH.org

Rape, Abuse and Incest National Network, RAINN.org

Trauma Survivors Network, Traumasurvivorsnetwork.org

HELP WITH FAMILY-RELATED ISSUES

DivorceCare, Divorcecare.com

National Parent Helpline, 855-427-2736 (855-4APARENT), Nationalparenthelpline.org

National Stepfamily Resource Center, Stepfamilies.info

Parents Without Partners (PWP), Parentswithoutpartners.org

GENERAL AND COMMUNITY SUPPORT

MenStuff: The National Men's Resource, Menstuff.org

PFLAG (Parents, Families, Friends, and Allies United with LGBTQ People), Community.pflag.org

United Way, Unitedway.org

LEGAL ASSISTANCE

American Bar Association, Americanbar.org

Self-Help

12-STEP GROUPS

Alcoholics Anonymous, AA.org

Cocaine Anonymous, CA.org

Gamblers Anonymous, Gamblersanonymous.org

Narcotics Anonymous, NA.org

Sexaholics Anonymous, SA.org

Sex and Love Addicts Anonymous, SLAAFWS.org

READING MATERIAL

Brinkman, Rick, and Rick Kirschner. *Dealing with People You Can't Stand: How to Bring Out the Best in People at Their Worst.* New York: McGraw-Hill, 2002.

Carter, Les, and Frank Minirth. *The Anger Trap: Free Yourself from the Frustrations That Sabotage Your Life.* San Francisco: Jossey-Bass, 2004.

Ellis, Albert. *How to Control Your Anger Before It Controls You.* New York: Citadel Press, 1997.

Guide to Self-Help Books, Guidetoselfhelpbooks.com

Huxley, Laura Archera. *You Are Not the Target.* New York: Farrar, Straus and Giroux, 1963.

McKay, Matthew. *When Anger Hurts: Quieting the Storm Within.* Oakland: New Harbinger Publications, 2003.

Psychology Today, Psychologytoday.com.

BIBLIOGRAPHY

Aamodt, S., and S. Wang. *Welcome to Your Child's Brain: How the Mind Grows from Conception to College.* New York: Bloomsbury, 2014.

Beck, R., and E. Fernandez. "Cognitive-Behavioral Therapy in the Treatment of Anger: A Meta-Analysis." *Cognitive Therapy and Research 2,* no. 1 (1998): 63–74. doi:10.1023/A:1018763902991.

Blum, Deborah. *Sex on the Brain.* New York: Viking Press, 1997.

Brizendine, Louann. *The Female Brain.* New York: Morgan Road Books, 2006.

Brizendine, Louann. *The Male Brain.* New York: Broadway Books, 2010.

Carter, Rita. *Mapping the Mind.* Berkeley: University of California Press, 1998.

Costandi, M. "Male Brain Versus Female Brain: How Do They Differ?" *The Guardian.* October 6, 2013. www.theguardian.com/science/neurophilosophy/2013/oct/06/male-brain-versus-female-brain. Accessed December 10, 2015.

Damasio, Antonio. *Descartes' Error: Emotion, Reason, and the Human Brain.* New York: Grosset/Putnam, 1994.

DiGiuseppe, R., and R. Tafrate. *Understanding Anger and Anger Disorders.* New York: Oxford University Press, 2007.

Gottman, John. *Why Marriages Succeed and Fail.* New York: Simon & Schuster, 1995.

Hamann, Stephan. "Sex Differences in Response to the Human Amygdala." *Neuroscientist* 11, no. 4 (2005): 288–93. doi:10.1177/1073858404271981.

Huxley, Aldous. *Texts and Pretexts: An Anthology with Commentaries.* London: Chatto & Windus, 1932.

Kassinove, H., and R. C. Tafrate. *Anger Management: The Complete Treatment Guide for Practitioners.* Atascadero, CA: Impact, 2002.

Kessler, R. C., E. F. Coccaro, M. Fava, S. Jaeger, and E. E. Walters. "The Prevalence and Correlates of DSM-IV Intermittent Explosive Disorder in the National Comorbidity Survey Replication." *Archives of General Psychiatry* 63, no. 6 (2006): 669–78. doi:10.1001/archpsyc.63.6.669.

LaVelle, H., S. Bore, D. Aslinia, and G. Morriss. "The Effects of Anger on the Brain and Body." *National Forum Journal of Counseling and Addiction* 2, no. 1 (2013): 1–12.

LeDoux, J. E. *The Emotional Brain: The Mysterious Underpinnings of Emotional Life.* New York: Simon & Schuster, 1996.

Martin, R. C., and E. R. Dahlen. "Irrational Beliefs and the Experience and Expression of Anger." *Journal of Rational-Emotive and Cognitive-Behavior Therapy* 22, no. 1 (2004): 3–20. doi:10.1023/B:JORE.0000011574.44362.8f.

Moir, Anne, and David Jessel. *Brain Sex: The Real Difference between Men and Women.* New York: Dell Publishing, 1992.

Niehoff, D. "Not Hardwired: The Complex Neurobiology of Sex Differences in Violence." *Violence and Gender* 1, no. 1 (2014): 19–24. doi:10.1089/vio.2013.0001.

Passamonti, L., M. Crockett, A. Apergis-Schoute, L. Clark, J. Rowe, A. Calder, and T. Robbins. "Effects of Acute Tryptophan Depletion on Prefrontal-Amygdala Connectivity While Viewing Facial Signals of Aggression." *Biological Psychiatry* 71, no. 1 (2012): 36–43. doi:10.1016/j.biopsych.2011.07.033.

Smith, T., K. Glazer, J. Ruiz, and L. Gallo. "Hostility, Anger, Aggressiveness, and Coronary Heart Disease: An Interpersonal Perspective on Personality, Emotion, and Health." *Journal of Personality* 72, no. 6 (2004): 1217–70. doi:10.1111/j.1467-6494.2004.00296.x.

Snell, W. E., S. Gum, R. L. Shuck, J. A. Mosley, and T. L. Hite, "The Clinical Anger Scale: Preliminary Reliability and Validity," *Journal of Clinical Psychology* 51 (1995), 215–26. doi:10.13072/midss.627.

Thomas, S. P. "Teaching Healthy Anger Management." *Perspectives in Psychiatric Care* 37 (2001): 41–48. doi:10.1111/j.1744-6163.2001.tb00617.x.

Williams, R. "Young Brains Lack Skills for Sharing." *Scientific American Mind* 23, no. 3 (2012), www.scientificamerican.com/article.cfm?id=young-brains-lack-skills-sharing.

INDEX

ACKNOWLEDGMENTS

I would like to thank all my instructors and colleagues who, throughout my educational and professional career, have believed in my abilities. I would like to acknowledge Dr. Nathan Hydes, who as a good friend was willing to give his time in assisting me with this book. I would like to recognize my friends Brad, Nick, and Jacob, who have shared their humor and best wishes during my most trying moments in life. I would like to thank my children, August and Lucinda, who are always cheering me on and inspiring me to push my comfort zone. I am extremely grateful for my mother, Louise; my sister, Jen; my stepmother, Ginny; my stepfather, Sal; my mother-in-law, Gay; my father-in-law, Denny; and my brother-in-law, Chad. They have all encouraged and supported me. And most of all, I am grateful for my adoring, thoughtful, and kind wife, Tara, whose love, efforts, and energy are appreciated beyond words. Thank you.

ABOUT THE AUTHOR & FOREWORD AUTHOR

AARON KARMIN is a licensed clinical professional counselor and certified clinical hypnotherapist in private practice at Urban Balance, Chicago. He earned his master's degree in clinical professional psychology from Roosevelt University. As a counselor, he has been helping his clients with anger management for more than 12 years, using an approach that focuses on increasing tolerance for frustration and developing control over impulsive behavior. As a hypnotherapist, he holds an advanced certification in stress management, which involves teaching six mind-body techniques to enhance relaxation. In addition to private practice, Aaron's experience includes service in outpatient as well as inpatient settings, community work, and counseling in nonprofit organizations and Fortune 500 companies. As a frequent guest lecturer and group therapy leader, he also deals with a variety of topics other than anger management and relaxation techniques, including communication skills and goal-setting strategies. In all his work, he recognizes the need for flexibility and creativity in addressing the mind and body, and he uses solution-based instructions to promote a healthy lifestyle.

NATHAN R. HYDES earned his BA in psychology from Northwest Nazarene University and his PhD in clinical psychology from Illinois Institute of Technology. He served a clinical internship at the National Center for PTSD in Boston and completed postdoctoral work at the Veterans Affairs hospital in North Little Rock, Arkansas. For the last five years, he has been on active duty as a psychologist in the US Navy.